Scottish
Highland
Knits

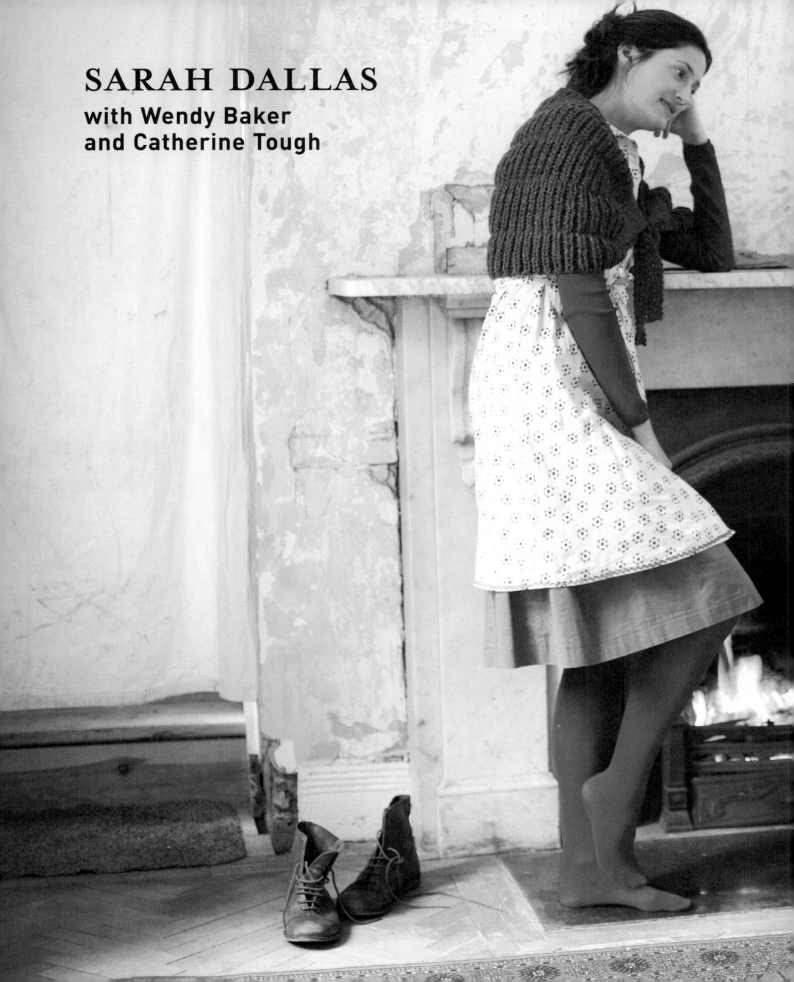

SARAH DALLAS

with Wendy Baker
and Catherine Tough

Scottish Highland Knits

T

TRAFALGAR SQUARE
North Pomfret, Vermont

SCOTTISH HIGHLAND KNITS

First published in the United States of America
in 2007 by Trafalgar Square Books
North Pomfret, Vermont 05053

Printed in Singapore

First published in Great Britain by Rowan Yarns as
Scottish Inspirations
Copyright © Rowan Yarns 2006

Editor Susan Berry
Designer Anne Wilson
Photographer John Heseltine
Stylist Emma Freemantle
Pattern writers Sue Whiting, Penny Hill and Eva Yates
Pattern checkers Stella Smith and Marilyn Wilson
Diagrams Stella Smith

Library of Congress Control Number: 2007927437

ISBN: 978-1-57076-377-9

Contents

Introduction

I have enjoyed the opportunity to collaborate with two colleagues on this book, Wendy Baker and Catherine Tough, both of them former students of mine in the School of Fashion Textiles at the Royal College of Art in London, where I am senior tutor, and both now established designers in their own right. Wendy and Catherine work in a similar way to me. They love subtlety of color, clarity, and simplicity of design, and attention to detail.

We also share a desire to make the most of the natural qualities of the yarn, in this case Rowan's *Scottish Tweed*. Inspired by the hand-dyed yarns of the Scottish Islands, it is robust yet subtle, with flecks of color and soft shades. The influence of nature can be seen in the color palette we have chosen: the grays and blacks of stones, the greens and browns of trees, wood, and leaves, with the odd flash of contrasting color, such as a heathery mauve.

The Fair Isle designs of Scotland need no introduction to knitters, but we chose in this book to give tradition a contemporary twist. The Fair Isles here are monochromatic—grays, whites, and blacks—and very simple. Just a hint of pattern here and there, to bring to life simple shapes. We also created designs that exploit the great texture of this pure wool yarn, choosing stitches such as cables and seed stitch.

Modern life makes particular demands on us all, and more and more we are looking for a balance between the frenetic urban environment and a desire for the slower pace of the countryside. So the pieces that we have created for this book reflect contemporary lifestyle needs: they are modern in style and shape, yet comforting and relaxing to touch and wear.

We have included a variety of knits: for men, women, and children, and for the home. I hope you enjoy knitting them as much as we enjoyed creating them!

SARAH DALLAS

About the designs

The following is a visual reference to the designs created by the three designers, Sarah Dallas, Wendy Baker, and Catherine Tough.

SARAH DALLAS

Seed stitch jacket
Rowan *Scottish Tweed Chunky*
Pages 10–14

Lace top
Rowan *Scottish Tweed 4 ply*
Pages 20–23

Wrap cardigan
Rowan *Scottish Tweed 4 ply*
Pages 24–29

Fair Isle scarf
Rowan *Scottish Tweed 4 ply*
Pages 30–33

Fair Isle stripe throw
Rowan *Scottish Tweed DK*
Pages 34–37

Fair Isle gloves
Rowan *Scottish Tweed 4 ply*
Pages 38–41

Fair Isle stripe cushion
Rowan *Scottish Tweed DK*
Pages 52–55

Chunky stripe cushion
Rowan *Scottish Tweed Chunky*
Pages 56–59

Fair Isle socks
Rowan *Scottish Tweed 4 ply*
Pages 70–73

Cabled blanket coat

Rowan *Scottish Tweed DK*

Pages 74–78

Man's Fair Isle sweater

Rowan *Scottish Tweed DK*

Pages 16–19

WENDY BAKER

Man's cabled sweater

Rowan *Scottish Tweed Chunky*

Pages 46–51

Tie shrug

Rowan *Scottish Tweed 4 ply*

Pages 82–84

Textured scarf

Rowan *Scottish Tweed 4 ply*

Pages 80–81

Collared jacket

Rowan *Scottish Tweed Aran*

Pages 86–90

CATHERINE TOUGH

Felted slippers

Rowan *Scottish Tweed DK*

Pages 42–45

Patchwork throw

Rowan *Scottish Tweed DK*

Pages 60–65

Child's jacket

Rowan *Scottish Tweed DK and 4 ply*

Pages 66–69

Seed stitch jacket

SARAH DALLAS

Sizes

	XS–S	M–L	XL–XXL	
To fit bust	32–34	36–38	40–42	in
	81–86	91–97	102–107	cm
Finished measurements				
Around bust	42	46½	50¾	in
	107	118	129	cm
Length to back neck	21¼	22	22¾	in
	54	56	58	cm
Sleeve seam	14½	15	15½	in
	37	38	39	cm

Yarns

9 (10: 11) x 100g/3½oz balls of Rowan *Scottish Tweed Chunky* in main color **MC** (Lewis Grey 007) and one ball in **A** (Midnight 023)

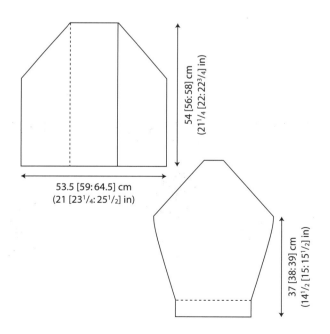

53.5 [59: 64.5] cm
(21 [23¼: 25½] in)

54 [56: 58] cm
(21¼ [22: 22¾] in)

37 [38: 39] cm
(14½ [15: 15½] in)

Needles

Pair of size 11 (8mm) knitting needles

Gauge

11 sts and 19 rows to 4in/10cm measured over seed st using size 11 (8mm) needles *or size to obtain correct gauge.*

Abbreviations

See page 93.

BACK

Using size 11 (8mm) needles and A, cast on 59 (65: 71) sts.

Break off A and join in MC.

Row 1 (RS) K1, *P1, K1; rep from * to end.

Row 2 Rep row 1.

These 2 rows form seed st.

Work in seed st until Back measures 13 (13¼: 13¾)in/ 33 (34: 35)cm from cast-on edge, ending with RS facing for next row.

Shape raglan armholes

Place markers at both ends of last row to denote base of armholes.

M–L and XL–XXL sizes only

Next row (RS) K1, skp, seed st to last 3 sts, K2tog, K1.

Next row P1, P2tog, seed st to last 3 sts, P2tog tbl, P1. (61: 67) sts.

Rep last 2 rows (0: 2) times more. (61: 59) sts.

All sizes

Next row (RS) K1, skp, seed st to last 3 sts, K2tog, K1. 57 (59: 57) sts.

Next row P2, seed st to last 2 sts, P2.

Rep last 2 rows 19 (19: 18) times more. 19 (21: 21) sts. Break off yarn and leave sts on a holder.

LEFT FRONT

Using size 11 (8mm) needles and A, cast on 39 (42: 45) sts.

Break off A and join in MC.

Row 1 (RS) *K1, P1; rep from * to last 1 (0: 1) st, K1 (0: 1).

Row 2 K1 (0: 1), *P1, K1; rep from * to end.

These 2 rows form seed st.

Work in seed st until Left Front matches Back to start of raglan armhole shaping, ending with RS facing for next row.

Shape raglan armhole

Place markers at end of last row to denote base of armholes.

Working all raglan armhole decreases in same way as for Back, dec 1 st at marked edge of next 1 (3: 7) rows, then on foll 19 (19: 18) alt rows. 19 (20: 20) sts.

Work 1 row, ending with RS facing for next row.

Break off yarn and leave sts on a holder.

RIGHT FRONT

Using size 11 (8mm) needles and A, cast on 39 (42: 45) sts.

Break off A and join in MC.

Row 1 (RS) K1 (0: 1), *P1, K1; rep from * to end.

Row 2 *K1, P1; rep from * to last 1 (0: 1) st, K1 (0: 1).

These 2 rows form seed st.

Complete to match Left Front, reversing shapings.

Do NOT break off yarn—set this ball of yarn aside as it will be used for Collar.

SLEEVES

Using size 11 (8mm) needles and A, cast on 31 (33: 35) sts.

Break off A and join in MC.

Work in seed st as given for Back, inc 1 st at each end of 19th row and every foll 6th row until there are 43 sts, then on every foll 8th row until there are 49 (51: 53) sts, taking inc sts into seed st.

Work even until Sleeve measures 17 (17¼: 17¾)in/ 43 (44: 45)cm from cast-on edge, ending with RS facing for next row.

Shape raglan

Place markers at both ends of last row to denote base of armholes.

Working all raglan decreases in same way as for Back raglan armhole, dec 1 st at each end of next row and every foll alt row until 9 sts rem.

Work 1 row, ending with RS facing for next row.

Break off yarn and leave sts on a holder.

FINISHING

Press lightly on WS following instructions on yarn label.

Sew raglan seams.

Collar

With RS facing, using size 11 (8mm) needles and ball of MC left with Right Front, work across Right Front sts as foll—seed st 16 (17: 17) sts, K2tog, K1, place marker on needle; work across sts of Right Sleeve as foll—K1, skp, seed st 3 sts, K2tog, K1, place marker on needle; work across sts of Back as foll—K1, skp, seed st 13 (15: 15) sts, K2tog, K1, place marker on needle; work across sts of Left Sleeve as foll—K1, skp, seed st 3 sts, K2tog, K1, place marker on needle; then work across Left Front sts as foll—K1, skp, seed st to end. 67 (71: 71) sts.

Row 1 (WS) [Seed st to within 2 sts of marker, P1, K2tog and move marker onto this st, P1] 4 times, seed st to end. 63 (67: 67) sts.

Row 2 [Seed st to within 1 st of marked st, sl 1, K2tog (marked st is first of these 2 sts), psso] 4 times, seed st to end. 55 (59: 59) sts.

Work in seed st as set for 13 rows, ending with RS facing for next row.

Row 16 Seed st 15 (16: 16) sts, sl 1, K2tog, psso, seed st 19 (21: 21) sts, sl 1, K2tog, psso, seed st to end. 51 (55: 55) sts.

Work in seed st for 3 rows more, ending with RS facing for next row.

Bind off in seed st.

Sew side and sleeve seams, reversing sleeve seam for first 2¾in/7cm for turn-back. Fold 2¼in/6cm cuff to RS.

Man's Fair Isle sweater

WENDY BAKER

Sizes

	S–M	L–XL	XXL–XXXL	
To fit chest	38–40	42–44	46–48	in
	97–102	107–112	117–122	cm
Finished measurements				
Around chest	42¼	46½	50¾	in
	107	118	129	cm
Length to shoulder	25¼	26	26¾	in
	64	66	68	cm
Sleeve seam	20½	20¾	21¼	in
	52	53	54	cm

Yarns

Rowan *Scottish Tweed DK*:

MC Storm Grey 004   12 (14: 15) x 50g/1¾oz balls
A   Lewis Grey 007   1 (1: 1) x 50g/1¾oz balls
B   Grey Mist 001   1 (1: 1) x 50g/1¾oz balls

Needles

Pair of size 5 (3.75mm) knitting needles
Pair of size 6 (4mm) knitting needles

Gauge

22 sts and 30 rows to 4in/10cm measured over
St st using size 6 (4mm) needles *or size to obtain
correct gauge.*

Abbreviations

See page 93.

Special abbreviation

Tw2 = K2tog leaving sts on left needle, K first st again
and slip both sts off left needle together.

Special note

When working patt in St st from chart, strand yarn not
in use loosely across WS of work, weaving it in every
3 or 4 sts. Work odd-numbered rows as K rows,
reading them from right to left, and even-numbered
rows as P rows, reading them from left to right.

BACK

Using size 5 (3.75mm) needles and A, cast on 118 (130:
142) sts.
Row 1 (RS) P2, *K2, P2; rep from * to end.
Row 2 K2, *P2, K2; rep from * to end.
Row 3 P2, *Tw2, P2; rep from * to end.
Row 4 Rep row 2.
These 4 rows form fancy rib.
Break off A and join in MC.
Work in fancy rib for 24 rows more, dec 1 st at end of
last row and ending with RS facing for next row.
117 (129: 141) sts.
Change to size 6 (4mm) needles.
Starting with a K row, work in St st until Back
measures 16 (16½: 17)in/41 (42: 43)cm from cast-on
edge, ending with RS facing for next row.

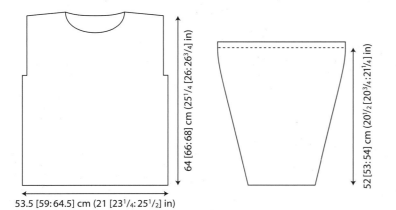

53.5 [59: 64.5] cm (21 [23¼: 25½] in)

64 [66:68] cm (25¼ [26:26¾] in)

52 [53: 54] cm (20½ [20¾:21¼] in)

Shape armholes

Bind off 6 sts at beg of next 2 rows. 105 (117: 129) sts.

Work even until armhole measures 4 (4¼: 4¾)in/ 10 (11: 12)cm, ending with RS facing for next row.

Place chart

Starting and ending rows as indicated, now work patt in St st from chart, working chart rows 1 to 42 once and then completing work in St st using MC only if required, as foll:

Work even until armhole measures 8¼ (8¾: 9)in/ 21 (22: 23)cm, ending with RS facing for next row.

Shape back neck

Next row (RS) Patt 34 (39: 43) sts and turn, leaving rem sts on a holder.

Work each side of neck separately.

Keeping patt correct, dec 1 st at neck edge of next 4 rows. 30 (35: 39) sts.

Work 1 row, ending with RS facing for next row.

Shape shoulder

Bind off 10 (12: 13) sts at beg of next and foll alt row.

Work 1 row.

Bind off rem 10 (11: 13) sts.

With RS facing, rejoin yarn to rem sts, bind off center 37 (39: 43) sts, patt to end.

Complete to match first side, reversing shapings.

FRONT

Work as given for Back until 18 (20: 22) rows less have been worked than on Back to start of shoulder shaping, ending with RS facing for next row.

Shape neck

Next row (RS) Patt 44 (50: 55) sts and turn, leaving rem sts on a holder.

Work each side of neck separately.

Keeping patt correct, dec 1 st at neck edge of next 13 rows, then on foll 1 (2: 3) alt rows. 30 (35: 39) sts.

Work 2 rows, ending with RS facing for next row.

Shape shoulder

Bind off 10 (12: 13) sts at beg of next and foll alt row.

Work 1 row.

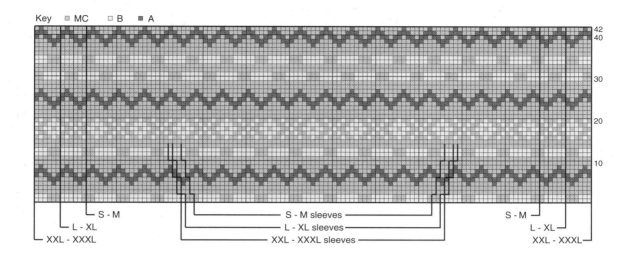

Key ■ MC □ B ■ A

S - M
L - XL
XXL - XXXL

S - M sleeves
L - XL sleeves
XXL - XXXL sleeves

S - M
L - XL
XXL - XXXL

Bind off rem 10 (11: 13) sts.

With RS facing, rejoin yarn to rem sts, bind off center 17 (17: 19) sts, patt to end.

Complete to match first side, reversing shapings.

SLEEVES

Using size 5 (3.75mm) needles and A, cast on 54 (58: 62) sts.

Work in fancy rib as given for Back for 4 rows.

Break off A and join in MC.

Work in fancy rib for 16 rows more, inc (inc: dec) 1 st at end of last row and ending with RS facing for next row. 55 (59: 61) sts.

Change to size 6 (4mm) needles.

Place chart

Starting and ending rows as indicated, now work in patt from chart as foll:

Inc 1 st at each end of 3rd row and 2 foll 4th rows. 61 (65: 67) sts.

Work 3 rows, ending after chart row 14 and with RS facing for next row.

Break off contrasting yarns and cont using MC **only**.

Starting with a K row, work in St st, shaping sides by inc 1 st at each end of next row and every foll 4th row until there are 89 (91: 95) sts, then on every foll 6th row until there are 107 (111: 115) sts.

Work even until Sleeve measures 20½ (20¾: 21¼)in/ 52 (53: 54)cm from cast-on edge, ending with RS facing for next row.

Top of sleeve

Place markers at both ends of last row.

Work 8 rows more, ending with RS facing for next row.

Bind off.

FINISHING

Press lightly on WS following instructions on yarn label and avoiding ribbing.

Sew right shoulder seam.

Collar

With RS facing, using size 5 (3.75mm) needles and MC, pick up and knit 18 (20: 22) sts down left front neck edge, 17 (17: 19) sts along center front neck edge, 18 (20: 22) sts up right front neck edge, then 57 (57: 59) sts across back neck edge. 110 (114: 122) sts.

Starting with a P row, work in St st until Collar measures 2¼in/6cm from pick-up row, ending with **WS** of body facing for next row.

Starting with row 1 (to reverse RS of work), now work in fancy rib as given for Back for 16 rows, ending with RS of Collar (WS of body) facing for next row.

Break off MC and join in A.

Work in fancy rib for 4 rows more.

Bind off in patt.

Sew left shoulder and Collar seam, reversing collar seam for turn-back. Matching sleeve markers to top of side seams and center of sleeve bound-off edge to shoulder seams, sew Sleeves to armholes. Sew side and sleeve seams.

Lace top

SARAH DALLAS

Sizes

XS	S	M	L	XL	XXL	
To fit bust						
32	34	36	38	40	42	in
81	86	91	97	102	107	cm
Finished measurements						
Around bust						
31	33½	36¼	38½	41	43¼	in
79	85	92	98	104	110	cm
Length to shoulder						
20	20½	20¾	21¼	21½	22	in
51	52	53	54	55	56	cm

Yarns

5 (6: 6: 7: 8: 8) x 25g/⅞oz balls of Rowan *Scottish Tweed 4 ply* in main color **MC** (Porridge 024), and one ball each in **A** (Lewis Grey 007) and **B** (Grey Mist 001)

Needles

Pair of size 3 (3mm) knitting needles
Pair of size 5 (3.75mm) knitting needles
Size 3 (3mm) circular knitting needle
Size E-4 (3.5mm) crochet hook

Extras

48in/120cm of narrow ribbon

Gauge

26 sts and 32 rows to 4in/10cm measured over patt using size 5 (3.75mm) needles *or size to obtain correct gauge.*

Abbreviations

See page 93.

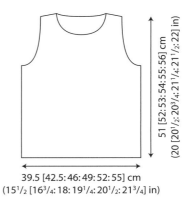

39.5 [42.5: 46: 49: 52: 55] cm
(15½ [16¾: 18: 19¼: 20½: 21¾] in)

51 [52: 53: 54: 55: 56] cm
(20 [20½: 20¾: 21¼: 21½: 22] in)

BACK

Using size 3 (3mm) needles and A, cast on 103 (111: 119: 127: 135: 143) sts.

Break off A and join in MC.

Rib row 1 (RS) K1, *P1, K1; rep from * to end.

Rib row 2 P1, *K1, P1; rep from * to end.

These 2 rows form rib.

Work in rib for 9 rows more, ending with **WS** facing for next row.

Change to size 5 (3.75mm) needles.

Now work in patt as foll:

Row 1 (WS) K2, P3, K2, *P1, K2, P3, K2; rep from * to end.

Row 2 P2, yo, sl 1, K2tog, psso, yo, P2, *K1, P2, yo, sl 1, K2tog, psso, yo, P2; rep from * to end.

Row 3 Rep row 1.

Row 4 P2, K1, yo, skp, P2, *K1, P2, K1, yo, skp, P2; rep from * to end.

Row 5 Rep row 1.

Row 6 P2, K3, P2, *K1, P2, K3, P2; rep from * to end.

These 6 rows form patt.

Cont in patt until Back measures 13 (13¼: 13¼: 13¾: 13¾: 14)in/33 (34: 34: 35: 35: 36)cm, ending with RS facing for next row.

Shape armholes

Keeping patt correct, bind off 4 (5: 5: 6: 6: 7) sts at beg of next 2 rows. 95 (101: 109: 115: 123: 129) sts.

Dec 1 st at each end of next 5 (7: 9: 11: 13: 15) rows, then on foll 7 alt rows. 71 (73: 77: 79: 83: 85) sts.**

Work even until armhole measures 7 (7: 7½: 7½: 7¾: 7¾)in/18 (18: 19: 19: 20: 20)cm, ending with RS facing for next row.

Shape back neck and shoulders

Next row (RS) Bind off 4 (4: 3: 3: 5: 5) sts, patt until there are 14 (14: 17: 17: 17: 18) sts on right needle and turn, leaving rem sts on a holder.

Work each side of neck separately.

Keeping patt correct, bind off 2 sts at beg of next row, 3 (3: 4: 4: 4: 5) sts at beg of foll row, 2 sts at beg of next row, then 3 (3: 4: 4: 4: 4) sts at beg of foll row.

Dec 1 st at neck edge of next row.

Bind off rem 3 (3: 4: 4: 4: 4) sts.

With RS facing, rejoin yarn to rem sts, bind off center 35 (37: 37: 39: 39: 39) sts, patt to end.

Complete to match first side, reversing shapings.

FRONT

Work as given for Back to **.

Work 3 (1: 3: 1: 3: 1) rows, ending with RS facing for next row.

Shape neck

Next row (RS) Patt 28 (28: 30: 30: 32: 33) sts and turn, leaving rem sts on a holder.

Work each side of neck separately.

Keeping patt correct, dec 1 st at neck edge of next 8 rows, then on foll 7 alt rows. 13 (13: 15: 15: 17: 18) sts.

Work even until Front matches Back to start of shoulder shaping, ending with RS facing for next row.

Shape shoulder

Bind off 4 (4: 3: 3: 5: 5) sts at beg of next row, 3 (3: 4: 4: 4: 5) sts at beg of foll alt row, then 3 (3: 4: 4: 4: 4) sts at beg of foll alt row.

Work 1 row.

Bind off rem 3 (3: 4: 4: 4: 4) sts.

With RS facing, rejoin yarn to rem sts, bind off center

15 (17: 17: 19: 19: 19) sts, patt to end.

Complete to match first side, reversing shapings.

FINISHING

Press lightly on WS following instructions on yarn label and avoiding ribbing.

Sew shoulder seams.

Neckband

With RS facing, using size 3 (3mm) circular needle and MC, starting and ending at left shoulder seam, pick up and knit 34 (33: 33: 32: 32: 32) sts down left front neck edge, 16 (16: 16: 18: 18: 18) sts along center front neck edge, 34 (33: 33: 32: 32: 32) sts up right front neck edge, then 56 (58: 58: 58: 58: 58) sts across back neck edge. 140 sts.

Rounds 1 and 2 Knit.

Round 3 K3 (2: 2:2: 2: 2), *yo, K2tog, K5; rep from * to last 4 (5: 5: 5: 5: 5) sts, yo, K2tog, K2 (3: 3: 3: 3: 3).

Rounds 4 and 5 Knit.

Bind off knitwise.

Neck edging

With RS facing, using size E-4 (3.5mm) crochet hook and B, join yarn with a slip st to bound-off edge of Neckband above one shoulder seam and work around neck edge as foll: ch 1 (does NOT count as st), 1 sc in bound-off st where yarn was joined on, *ch 5, 1 slip st in last sc, 1 sc in each of next 4 bound-off sts; rep from * to last 3 bound-off sts, ch 5, 1 slip st in last sc, 1 sc in each of last 3 bound-off sts, join with a slip st to first sc.

Fasten off.

Armhole borders (both alike)

With RS facing, using size 3 (3mm) needles and MC, pick up and knit 105 (105: 109: 119: 113: 113) sts evenly all around armhole edge.

Work in rib as given for Back for 5 rows, ending with RS facing for next row.

Break off MC and join in B.

Bind off in rib.

Sew side and Armhole Border seams. Starting and ending either side of center front, thread ribbon through round 3 of Neckband and tie in bow at front.

Wrap cardigan
SARAH DALLAS

Sizes

	XS–S	M–L	XL–XXL	
To fit bust	32–34	36–38	40–42	in
	81–86	91–97	102–107	cm
Finished measurements				
Around bust	36½	40½	44½	in
	93	103	113	cm
Length to shoulder	15½	16½	17¼	in
	39	42	44	cm
Sleeve seam	18	18½	19	in
	46	47	48	cm

Yarns

10 (12: 13) x 25g/⁷⁄₈oz balls of Rowan *Scottish Tweed 4 ply* in main color **MC** (Lavender 005), and one ball each in **A** (Apple 015) and **B** (Brilliant Pink 010)

Needles

Pair of size 3 (3.25mm) knitting needles
Pair of size 5 (3.75mm) knitting needles
Size D-3 (3mm) crochet hook

Gauge

24 sts and 32 rows to 4in/10cm measured over patt using size 5 (3.75mm) needles *or size to obtain correct gauge.*

Abbreviations

See page 93.

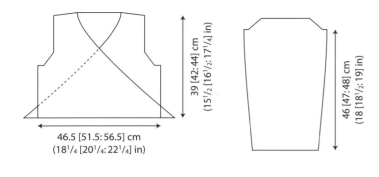

46.5 [51.5:56.5] cm
(18¹/₄ [20¹/₄:22¹/₄] in)

39 [42:44] cm
(15¹/₂ [16¹/₂:17¹/₄] in)

46 [47:48] cm
(18 [18¹/₂:19] in)

BACK

Using size 3 (3.25mm) needles and A, cast on 111 (123: 135) sts.

Break off A and join in MC.

Rib row 1 (RS) K1, *P1, K1; rep from * to end.

Rib row 2 P1, *K1, P1; rep from * to end.

These 2 rows form rib.

Work in rib for 4 rows more, ending with RS facing for next row.

Change to size 5 (3.75mm) needles.

Now work in patt as foll:

Row 1 (RS) Knit.

Row 2 and every foll alt row Purl.

Row 3 K3 (1: 7), *yo, skp, K6; rep from * to last 4 (2: 8) sts, yo, skp, K2 (0: 6).

Row 5 K1 (2: 5), [yo, skp, K3] 0 (1: 0) times, *K2tog, yo, K1, yo, skp, K3; rep from * to last 6 (4: 2) sts, [K2tog, yo] 1 (1: 0) times, [K1, yo, skp] 1 (0: 0) times, K1 (2: 2).

Row 7 Rep row 3.

Row 9 Knit.

Row 11 K7 (5: 3), *yo, skp, K6; rep from * to last 8 (6: 4) sts, yo, skp, K6 (4: 2).

Row 13 K5 (3: 1), *K2tog, yo, K1, yo, skp, K3; rep from * to last 2 (0: 6) sts, [K2tog, yo, K1, yo, skp] 0 (0: 1) times, K2 (0: 1).

Row 15 Rep row 11.

Row 16 Rep row 2.

These 16 rows form patt.

Cont in patt for 44 (48: 52) rows more, ending with RS facing for next row.

Shape armholes

Keeping patt correct, bind off 5 (6: 7) sts at beg of next 2 rows. 101 (111: 121) sts.

M–L and XL–XXL sizes only

Next row (RS) K2, skp, patt to last 4 sts, K2tog, K2.

Next row P2, P2tog, P to last 4 sts, P2tog tbl, P2. (107: 117) sts.

XL–XXL size only

Rep last 2 rows once more. 113 sts.

All sizes

Next row (RS) K2, skp, patt to last 4 sts, K2tog, K2.

Next row Purl.

Rep last 2 rows 8 (9: 10) times more. 83 (87: 91) sts.

Work even until armhole measures 7¹/₂ (7³/₄: 8¹/₄)in/ 19 (20: 21)cm, ending with RS facing for next row.

Shape shoulders

Keeping patt correct, bind off 5 (5: 6) sts at beg of next 6 (4: 8) rows, then 6 (6: 0) sts at beg of foll 2 (4: 0) rows.

Bind off rem 41 (43: 43) sts.

LEFT FRONT

Using size 3 (3.25mm) needles and A, cast on 120 (132: 144) sts.

Break off A and join in MC.

Rib row 1 (RS) *K1, P1; rep from * to end.

Rib row 2 Rep row 1.

These 2 rows form rib.

Work in rib for 4 rows more, ending with RS facing for next row.

Change to size 5 (3.75mm) needles.

Now work in patt, shaping front slope, as foll:

Row 1 (RS) K to last 3 sts, K2tog, K1. 119 (131: 143) sts.

Row 2 and every foll alt row P1, P2tog, P to end.

Row 3 K3 (1: 7), *yo, skp, K6; rep from * to last 3 (9: 7) sts, [yo, skp] 0 (1: 1) times, K0 (4: 2), K2tog, K1. 117 (129: 141) sts.

Row 5 K1 (2: 5), [yo, skp, K3] 0 (1: 0) times, *K2tog, yo, K1, yo, skp, K3; rep from * to last 3 (9: 7) sts, [K2tog, yo] 0 (1: 1) times, [K1, yo, skp] 0 (1: 0) times, K0 (1: 2), K2tog, K1. 115 (127: 139) sts.

Row 7 K3 (1: 7), *yo, skp, K6; rep from * to last 7 (5: 11) sts, yo, skp, K2 (0: 6), K2tog, K1. 113 (125: 137) sts.

Row 9 Rep row 1. 111 (123: 135) sts.

Row 11 K7 (5: 3), *yo, skp, K6; rep from * to last 7 (5: 3) sts, [yo, skp] 1 (1: 0) times, K2 (0: 0), K2tog, K1. 109 (121: 133) sts.

Row 13 K5 (3: 1), *K2tog, yo, K1, yo, skp, K3; rep from * to last 7 (5: 3) sts, [K2tog, yo] 1 (0: 0) times, K2 (2: 0), K2tog, K1. 107 (119: 131) sts.

Row 15 K7 (5: 3), *yo, skp, K6; rep from * to last 11 (9: 7) sts, yo, skp, K6 (4: 2), K2tog, K1. 105 (117: 129) sts.

Row 16 Rep row 2. 104 (116: 128) sts.

These 16 rows form patt and start front slope shaping.

Cont in patt, dec 1 st at front slope edge of next 43 (48: 52) rows. 61 (68: 76) sts.

Work 1 (0: 0) row more, ending with RS facing for next row.

Shape armhole

Keeping patt correct, bind off 5 (6: 7) sts at beg and dec 1 st at end of next row. 55 (61: 68) sts.

Work 1 row.

Working all armhole decreases as set by Back, dec 1 st at armhole edge of next 1 (3: 5) rows, then on foll 8 (9: 10) alt rows **and at same time** dec 1 st at front slope edge of next row and every foll alt row. 37 (38: 40) sts.

Dec 1 st at front slope edge **only** of every foll alt row until 21 (22: 24) sts rem.

Work even until Left Front matches Back to start of shoulder shaping, ending with RS facing for next row.

Shape shoulder

Keeping patt correct, bind off 5 (5: 6) sts at beg of next row and foll 2 (1: 2) alt rows, then 0 (6: 0) sts at beg of foll 0 (1: 0) alt row.

Work 1 row.

Bind off rem 6 sts.

RIGHT FRONT

Using size 3 (3.25mm) needles and A, cast on 120 (132: 144) sts.

Break off A and join in MC.

Rib row 1 (RS) *P1, K1; rep from * to end.

Rib row 2 Rep row 1.

These 2 rows form rib.

Work in rib for 4 rows more, ending with RS facing for next row.

Change to size 5 (3.75mm) needles.

Now work in patt, shaping front slope, as foll:

Row 1 (RS) K1, skp, K to end. 119 (131: 143) sts.

Row 2 and every foll alt row P to last 3 sts, P2tog tbl, P1.

Row 3 K1, skp, K7 (5: 3), *yo, skp, K6; rep from * to last 4 (2: 8) sts, yo, skp, K2 (0: 6). 117 (129: 141) sts.

Row 5 K1, skp, K3 (1: 2), [yo, skp, K3] 0 (0: 1) times, *K2tog, yo, K1, yo, skp, K3; rep from * to last 6 (4: 2) sts, [K2tog, yo] 1 (1: 0) times, [K1, yo, skp] 1 (0: 0) times, K1 (2: 2). 115 (127: 139) sts.

Row 7 K1, skp, K3 (1: 7), *yo, skp, K6; rep from * to last 4 (2: 8) sts, yo, skp, K2 (0: 6). 113 (125: 137) sts.

Row 9 Rep row 1. 111 (123: 135) sts.

Row 11 K1, skp, K3 (1: 7), *yo, skp, K6; rep from * to last 8 (6: 4) sts, yo, skp, K6 (4: 2). 109 (121: 133) sts.

Row 13 K1, skp, K2 (0: 0), [yo, skp] 1 (1: 0) times, K3, *K2tog, yo, K1, yo, skp, K3; rep from * to last 2 (0: 6) sts, [K2tog, yo, K1, yo, skp] 0 (0: 1) times, K2 (0: 1). 107 (119: 131) sts.

Row 15 K1, skp, K7 (5: 3), *yo, skp, K6; rep from * to last 8 (6: 4) sts, yo, skp, K6 (4: 2). 105 (117: 129) sts.

Row 16 Rep row 2. 104 (116: 128) sts.

These 16 rows form patt and start front slope shaping.

Complete to match Left Front, reversing shapings.

SLEEVES

Using size 3 (3.25mm) needles and B, cast on 55 (59: 61) sts.

Break off B and join in MC.

Work in rib as given for Back for 2in/5cm, ending with RS facing for next row.

Change to size 5 (3.75mm) needles.

Now work in patt as foll:

Row 1 (RS) Knit.

Row 2 and every foll alt row Purl.

Row 3 K3 (5: 6), *yo, skp, K6; rep from * to last 4 (6: 7) sts, yo, skp, K2 (4: 5).

Row 5 K1 (3: 4), *K2tog, yo, K1, yo, skp, K3; rep from * to last 6 (0: 1) sts, [K2tog, yo, K1, yo, skp] 1 (0: 0) times, K1 (0: 1).

Row 7 Rep row 3.

Row 9 Knit.

Row 11 K7 (1: 2), *yo, skp, K6; rep from * to last 8 (2: 3) sts, yo, skp, K6 (0: 1).

Row 13 [Inc in first st] 0 (0: 1) times, K5 (2: 2), [yo, skp, K3] 0 (1: 1) times, *K2tog, yo, K1, yo, skp, K3; rep from * to last 2 (4: 5) sts, [K2tog, yo] 0 (1: 1) times, K2, [inc in last st] 0 (0: 1) times. 55 (59: 63) sts.

Row 15 [Inc in first st] 1 (1: 0) times, K6 (0: 3), *yo, skp, K6; rep from * to last 8 (10: 4) sts, yo, skp, K5 (7: 2), [inc in last st] 1 (1: 0) times. 57 (61: 63) sts.

Row 16 Rep row 2.

These 16 rows form patt and start sleeve shaping.

Cont in patt, shaping sides by inc 1 st at each end of 15th (15th: 11th) row and every foll 16th (16th: 14th) row until there are 65 (67: 67) sts, then on every foll 18th (18th: 16th) row until there are 69 (73: 77) sts, taking inc sts into patt.

Work even until Sleeve measures 18 (18½: 19)in/ 46 (47: 48)cm from cast-on edge, ending with RS facing for next row.

Shape top of sleeve

Keeping patt correct, bind off 5 (6: 7) sts at beg of next 2 rows. 59 (61: 63) sts.

Working all decreases as set by Back armhole decreases, dec 1 st at each end of next row and foll 7 (8: 9) alt rows. 43 sts.

Work 1 row, ending with RS facing for next row.

Bind off 2 sts at beg of next 6 rows.

Bind off rem 31 sts.

FINISHING

Press lightly on WS following instructions on yarn label and avoiding ribbing.

Sew shoulder seams.

Neck edging

With RS facing, using size D-3 (3mm) crochet hook and B, join yarn with a slip st to cast-on edge of Right Front at base of front slope shaping.

Working into row-end edges along front slopes and bound-off sts across back neck, work along entire front slope and back neck edge as foll: ch 1 (does NOT count as st), 1 sc in point where yarn was joined on, 1 sc in edge, *ch 3, 1 sc in same place as last sc, 2 sc in edge; rep from * to cast-on edge of Left Front. Fasten off.

Sew side seams. Sew sleeve seams. Sew Sleeves to armholes.

Fair Isle scarf

SARAH DALLAS

Size

The finished scarf measures 12¹⁄₂in/32cm by
54¹⁄₄in/138cm.

Yarns

5 x 25g/⁷⁄₈oz balls of Rowan *Scottish Tweed 4 ply* in
main color **MC** (Grey Mist 001), and one ball each in
A (Sunset 011), **B** (Lewis Grey 007), **C** (Porridge 024),
D (Midnight 023), and **E** (Brilliant Pink 010)

Needles

Pair of size 5 (3.75mm) knitting needles

Gauge

24 sts and 32 rows to 4in/10cm measured over
St st using size 5 (3.75mm) needles *or size to obtain
correct gauge.*

Abbreviations

See page 93.

Special note

When working patt from chart, strand yarn not in use
loosely across WS of work, weaving it in every 3 or
4 sts. Work odd-numbered rows as RS rows, reading
them from right to left, and even-numbered rows as
WS rows, reading them from left to right.

SCARF

Using size 5 (3.75mm) needles and A, cast on 77 sts.
Break off A and join in MC.

Row 1 (RS) [K1, P1] twice, K to last 4 sts, [P1, K1] twice.

Row 2 K1, P1, K1, P to last 3 sts, K1, P1, K1.

These 2 rows form patt.

Work in patt for 6 rows more, ending with RS facing for
next row.

Work first Fair Isle band

Joining in and breaking off B, C, and D as required,
work from chart as foll:

Work chart rows 1 to 12 three times, then rep chart
rows 1 to 9 again, ending with **WS** facing for next row.

Break off B, C, and D and cont using MC only.

Work even in patt until Scarf measures 52in/132cm
from cast-on edge, ending with RS facing for next row.

Work second Fair Isle band

Joining in and breaking off B, C, and D as required, work
chart rows 1 to 9, ending with **WS** facing for next row.

Break off B, C, and D and cont using MC only.

Work even in patt for 9 rows, ending with RS facing for
next row.

Break off MC and join in E.

Next row (RS) Using E, knit.

Bind off purlwise.

FINISHING

Press lightly on WS following instructions on yarn label.

Key

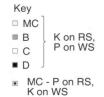

MC ⎤
B ⎤ K on RS,
C ⎦ P on WS
D

MC - P on RS,
K on WS

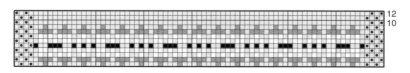

Fair Isle stripe throw

SARAH DALLAS

Size

The finished throw measures 51in/130cm by
67³/₄in/172cm.

Yarns

Rowan *Scottish Tweed DK*:

A	Grey Mist 001	10 x 50g/1³/₄oz balls
B	Storm Grey 004	10 x 50g/1³/₄oz balls
C	Lavender 005	1 x 50g/1³/₄oz ball
D	Lewis Grey 007	1 x 50g/1³/₄oz ball
E	Midnight 023	1 x 50g/1³/₄oz ball
F	Brilliant Pink 010	1 x 50g/1³/₄oz ball
G	Apple 015	1 x 50g/1³/₄oz ball

Needles

Pair of size 7 (4.5mm) knitting needles
Size G-6 (4mm) crochet hook

Gauge

20 sts and 26 rows to 4in/10cm measured over
St st using size 7 (4.5mm) needles *or size to obtain
correct gauge.*

Abbreviations

See page 93.

Special note

When working patt from chart, strand yarn not in use
loosely across WS of work, weaving it in every 3 or
4 sts. Work odd-numbered rows as RS rows, reading
them from right to left, and even-numbered rows as
WS rows, reading them from left to right.

FIRST STRIP

Using size 7 (4.5mm) needles and C, cast on 130 sts.

Break off C and join in A.

Row 1 (RS) Knit.

Row 2 K5, P to end.

These 2 rows form patt.

Work in patt until Strip measures 20in/51cm, ending with RS facing for next row.

Work Fair Isle band

Join in D.

Following chart A, work chart rows 1 to 11, ending with **WS** facing for next row.

Break off D and cont using A only.

Work even in patt until Strip measures 67¾in/172cm from cast-on edge, ending with **WS** facing for next row.

Break off A and join in F.

Next row (WS) Purl.

Bind off.

SECOND STRIP

Using size 7 (4.5mm) needles and C, cast on 130 sts.

Break off C and join in B.

Row 1 (RS) Knit.

Row 2 P to last 5 sts, K5.

These 2 rows form patt.

Work in patt until Strip measures 46½in/118cm, ending with RS facing for next row.

Work Fair Isle band

Join in E.

Following chart B, work chart rows 1 to 11, ending with **WS** facing for next row.

Break off E and cont using B only.

Work even in patt until Strip measures 67¾in/172cm from cast-on edge, ending with **WS** facing for next row.

Break off B and join in F.

Next row (WS) Purl.

Bind off.

FINISHING

Press lightly on WS following instructions on yarn label.

Join strips

Lay First Strip flat with WS uppermost, then lay Second Strip on top of First, with WS together and cast-on and bound-off edges matching.

Using size G-6 (4mm) crochet hook and G, join Strips by working a row of sc along central row-end edges, working each st through both layers. (Garter st borders of Strips form outer edges.)

Fasten off.

Key
□ A ⎫ K on RS,
▨ D ⎭ P on WS
▨ A - K on WS

ChartA

11

Key
▨ B ⎫ K on RS,
■ E ⎭ P on WS
▨ B - K on WS

ChartB

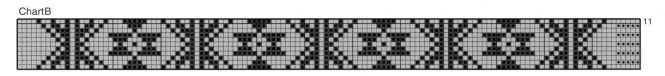

11

Fair Isle gloves

SARAH DALLAS

Size

The finished gloves measure 7¹/₂in/19cm around palm of hand.

Yarns

2 x 25g/⁷/₈oz balls of Rowan *Scottish Tweed 4 ply* in main color **MC** (Grey Mist 001), and one ball each in **A** (Midnight 023), **B** (Lewis Grey 007), and **C** (Porridge 024)

Needles

Set of four size 2 (2.75mm) double-pointed knitting needles

Gauge

32 sts and 36 rows to 4in/10cm measured over St st using size 2 (2.75mm) needles *or size to obtain correct gauge.*

Abbreviations

See page 93.

Special note

When working patt from chart, strand yarn not in use loosely across WS of work, weaving it in every 3 or 4 sts. Work ALL rounds as RS (knit) rounds, reading them from right to left.

RIGHT GLOVE

Using size 2 (2.75mm) double-pointed needles and A, cast on 60 sts, distributing them evenly over 3 needles. Break off A and join in MC.
Round 1 (RS) *K1, P1; rep from * to end.
This round forms rib.
Work in rib for 36 rounds more, ending with RS facing for next row.

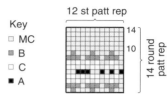

Round 38 [Rib 2, inc in next st, rib 2] 12 times. 72 sts. Joining in A, B, and C as required, repeating the 12 st patt rep 6 times around each round and repeating the 14 round patt rep throughout, start with chart row 1 and work from chart as foll:
Work 24 rounds.**

Shape thumb

Round 25 Slip first 18 sts of next round onto a safety pin, cast on 6 sts onto right needle, then patt rem 54 sts of round. 60 sts.
Keeping patt correct (by now repeating the 12 st patt rep 5 times around each round), work 13 rounds, ending after chart round 10.
Break off A, B, and C and cont in rounds of St st (K every round) using MC only.
Work 4 rounds.

Shape first finger

Next round K5, slip next 44 sts onto a holder, cast on 2 sts onto right needle, then K rem 11 sts. 18 sts.
***Distribute these 18 sts over 3 needles.
Work even until first finger measures 2³/₄in/7cm.
Next round [K2tog] 9 times. 9 sts.
Work 1 round.
Next round [K1, K2tog] 3 times.
Break off yarn and thread through rem 6 sts. Pull up tight and fasten off securely.

Shape second finger

Return to sts left on holder and work as foll:

Next round K first 8 sts on holder, leave next 28 sts on holder, cast on 2 sts onto right needle, K rem 8 sts from holder, then pick up and K 2 sts from base of first finger. 20 sts.

Distribute these 20 sts over 3 needles.

Work even until second finger measures 3in/7.5cm.

Next round [K2tog] 10 times. 10 sts.

Work 1 round.

Next round [K2tog] 5 times.

Break off yarn and thread through rem 5 sts. Pull up tight and fasten off securely.

Shape third finger

Return to sts left on holder and work as foll:

Next round K first 7 sts on holder, leave next 14 sts on holder, cast on 2 sts onto right needle, K rem 7 sts from holder, then pick up and K 2 sts from base of second finger. 18 sts.

Distribute these 18 sts over 3 needles.

Work even until third finger measures 2¾in/7cm.

Next round [K2tog] 9 times. 9 sts.

Work 1 round.

Next round [K1, K2tog] 3 times.

Break off yarn and thread through rem 6 sts. Pull up tight and fasten off securely.

Shape fourth finger

Return to sts left on holder and work as foll:

Next round K rem 14 sts on holder, then pick up and K 2 sts from base of third finger. 16 sts.

Distribute these 16 sts over 3 needles.

Work even until fourth finger measures 2¼in/6cm.

Next round [K2tog] 8 times. 8 sts.

Work 1 round.

Next round [K2tog, K1] twice, K2tog.

Break off yarn and thread through rem 5 sts. Pull up tight and fasten off securely.

Shape thumb

Return to sts left on safety pin and work as foll:

Next round K 18 sts from safety pin, then pick up and K 6 sts from base of palm. 24 sts.

Distribute these 24 sts over 3 needles.

Work even until thumb measures 2¼in/6cm.

Next round [K2tog] 12 times. 12 sts.

Work 1 round.

Next round [K2tog] 6 times.

Break off yarn and thread through rem 6 sts. Pull up tight and fasten off securely.

LEFT GLOVE

Work as given for Right Glove to **.

Shape thumb

Round 25 Patt 54 sts, slip rem 18 sts onto a safety pin, cast on 6 sts onto right needle. 60 sts.

Keeping patt correct (by now repeating the 12 st patt rep 5 times around each round), work 13 rounds, ending after chart round 10.

Break off A, B, and C and cont in rounds of St st (K every round) using MC only.

Work 4 rounds.

Shape first finger

Next round K11, slip next 44 sts onto a holder, cast on 2 sts onto right needle, then K rem 5 sts. 18 sts.

Complete as given for right glove from ***.

FINISHING

Press lightly following instructions on yarn label and avoiding ribbing.

Felted slippers
CATHERINE TOUGH

Size

The finished slippers measure 10½in/27cm from heel to toe.

Yarns

Rowan *Scottish Tweed DK*:

A	Storm Grey 004	1 x 50g/1¾oz balls
B	Grey Mist 001	1 x 50g/1¾oz balls
C	Rose 026	1 x 50g/1¾oz balls

Needles

Pair of size 8 (5mm) knitting needles

Extras

11¾in/30cm square piece of thin foam rubber and matching sewing thread

Gauge

Before felting: 17 sts and 26 rows to 4in/10cm measured over St st using size 8 (5mm) needles *or size to obtain correct gauge.*

Abbreviations

See page 93.

SOLE SECTIONS (make 2)

Using size 8 (5mm) needles and A, cast on 60 sts. Starting with a K row, work in St st for 29½in/75cm. Bind off.

UPPER SECTIONS (make 2)

Using size 8 (5mm) needles and B, cast on 70 sts. Starting with a K row, work in St st for 6in/15cm, ending with RS facing for next row. Join in C.

⊕ **SCOTTISH HIGHLAND KNITS**

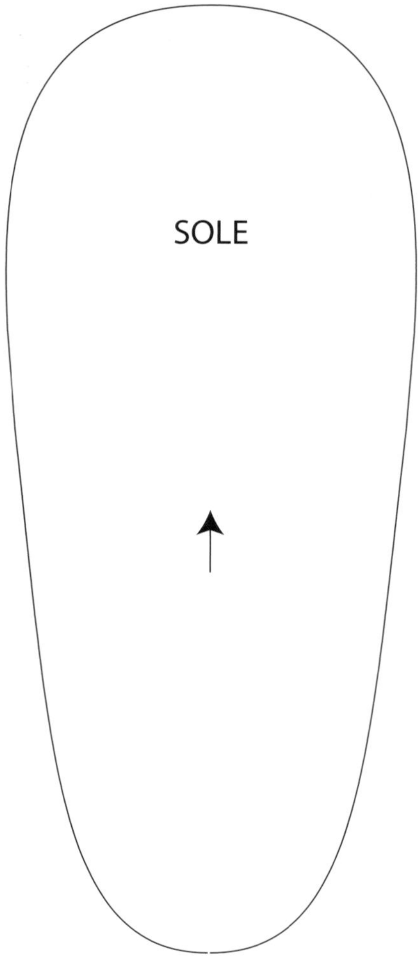

SOLE

TEMPLATES 50% OF ACTUAL SIZE

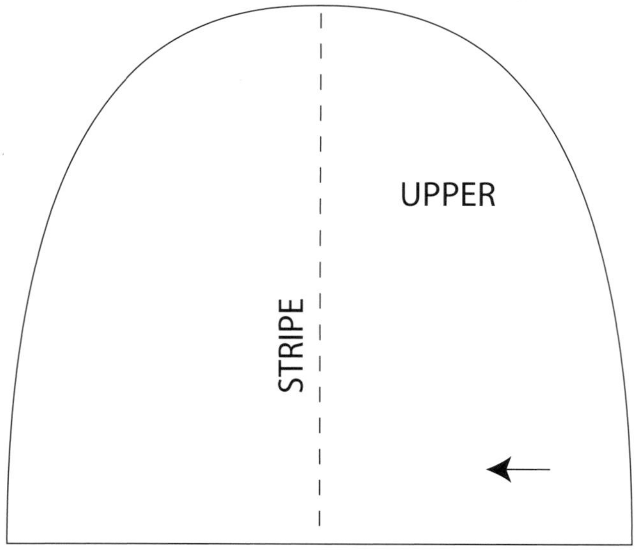

UPPER

STRIPE

← indicates direction of knitting

Using C, work in St st for 1 row.
Break off C.
Using B, and beg with a P row, cont in St st until
Section measures 6in/15cm from stripe in C.
Bind off.

FINISHING

Machine wash knitted pieces at 104°F/40° to shrink
and felt them. The fabric will shrink a little more each
time it is washed so repeat this process until either
you are happy with the felted effect created, or
sections have shrunk to their minimum size. Felted
Sole piece must be at least 11in/28cm by 23½in/60cm,
and felted Upper piece must be at least 13in/33cm by
6¼in/16cm.

Once felted pieces are dry, press carefully on WS.
Enlarge Sole and Upper templates. Using template,
cut out Sole shape 4 times from felted sole fabric, and
twice from foam rubber. Trim away ¼in/6mm from
outer edge of foam rubber sole pieces.

Using template, cut out Upper shape twice from felted
upper fabric, ensuring stripe falls along line indicated.
Machine stitch twice along straight (row end) edge of
Upper—firstly ¼in/6mm from edge, then again
between this line of stitching and cut edge.

For Sole, form a "sandwich" by placing one foam
rubber piece facing WS of one felted piece and
covering this with another felted sole piece, again with
WS of knitting facing foam rubber. Baste pieces
together around entire outer edge.

Lay Upper on Sole "sandwich", placing one end of
stripe at center of toe and matching cut edges along
side—Upper will stand away from Sole to allow foot
to fit into slipper. Baste upper in place along outer
curved edge.

Machine stitch twice around entire outer edge of Sole,
enclosing Upper in stitching—firstly stitch ¼in/6mm
from edge, then again between this line of stitching
and cut edge.

Man's cabled sweater

WENDY BAKER

Sizes

	S–M	L–XL	XXL–XXXL	
To fit chest	38–40	42–44	46–48	in
	97–102	107–112	117–122	cm
Finished measurements				
Around chest	48	52	56	in
	122	132	142	cm
Length to shoulder	26¾	27½	28¼	in
	68	70	72	cm
Sleeve seam	19¼	19½	20	in
	49	50	51	cm

Yarns

10 (12: 13) x 100g/3½oz balls of Rowan *Scottish Tweed Chunky* in Olive Green 035

Needles

Pair of size 10½ (7mm) knitting needles
Pair of size 11 (8mm) knitting needles
Cable needle

Gauge

12 sts and 16 rows to 4in/10cm measured over St st using size 11 (8mm) needles *or size to obtain correct gauge.*

Abbreviations

See page 93.

Special abbreviations

wyif = with yarn at front (RS) of work.
Cr4R = slip next st onto cable needle and leave at back of work, K3, then P1 from cable needle.
Cr4L = slip next 3 sts onto cable needle and leave at front of work, P1, then K3 from cable needle.
C6B = slip next 3 sts onto cable needle and leave at back of work, K3, then K3 from cable needle.
C6F = slip next 3 sts onto cable needle and leave at front of work, K3, then K3 from cable needle.

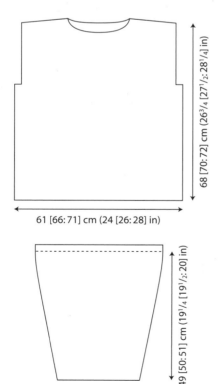

68 [70:72] cm (26¾ [27½:28¼] in)

61 [66:71] cm (24 [26:28] in)

49 [50:51] cm (19¼ [19½:20] in)

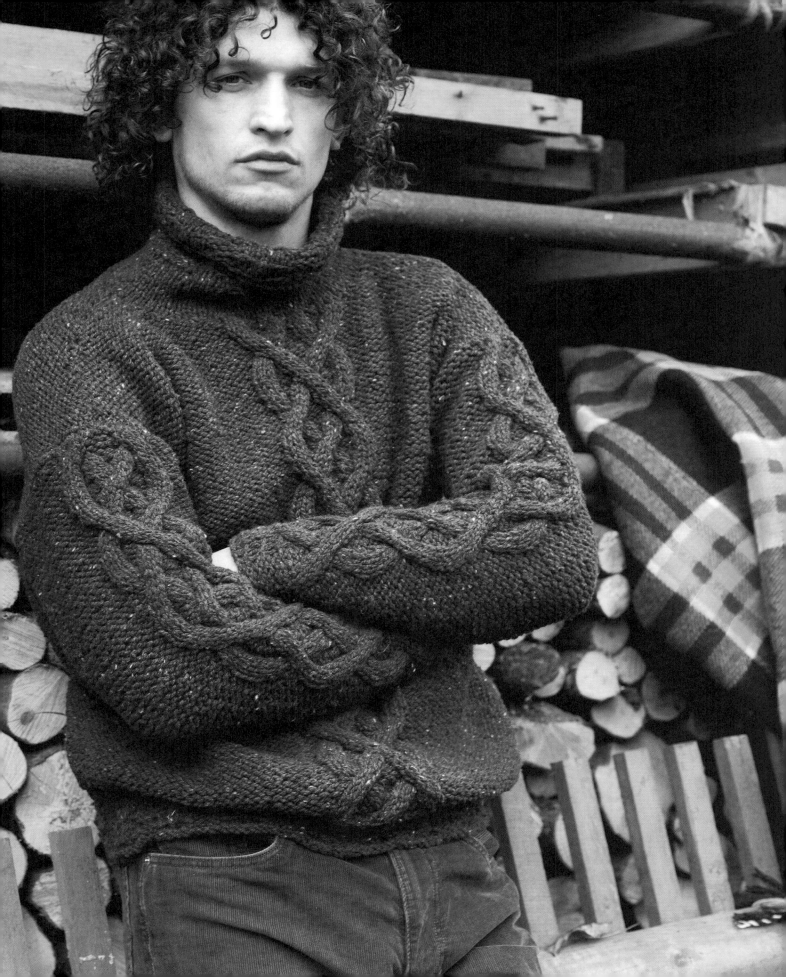

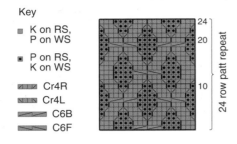

Key
- ▪ K on RS, P on WS
- ▫ P on RS, K on WS
- Cr4R
- Cr4L
- C6B
- C6F

24 row patt repeat

BACK

Using size 10½ (7mm) needles, cast on 73 (79: 85) sts.

Row 1 (WS) Purl.

Row 2 P2 (1: 4), *sl 5 wyif, P3; rep from * to last 7 (6: 9) sts, sl 5 wyif, P2 (1: 4).

Row 3 K2 (1: 4), *P5, K3; rep from * to last 7 (6: 9) sts, P5, K2 (1: 4).

Row 4 P2 (1: 4), *K2, insert tip of right needle under strand of yarn of row 2 then K next st, K2, P3; rep from * to last 7 (6: 9) sts, K2, insert tip of right needle under strand of yarn of row 2 then K next st, K2, P2 (1: 4).

These 4 rows form fancy rib.

Work in fancy rib for 13 rows more, ending with RS facing for next row.

Change to size 11 (8mm) needles.

Starting with a P row, work in rev St st until Back measures 17¼ (17¾: 18)in/44 (45: 46)cm from cast-on edge, ending with RS facing for next row.

Shape armholes

Bind off 4 sts at beg of next 2 rows. 65 (71: 77) sts.

Work even until armhole measures 9 (9½: 9¾)in/ 23 (24: 25)cm, ending with RS facing for next row.

Shape back neck

Next row (RS) P22 (24: 26) and turn, leaving rem sts on a holder.

Work each side of neck separately.

Dec 1 st at neck edge of next row, ending with RS facing for next row. 21 (23: 25) sts.

Shape shoulder

Bind off 10 (11: 12) sts at beg and dec 1 st at end of next row.

Work 1 row.

Bind off rem 10 (11: 12) sts.

With RS facing, rejoin yarn to rem sts, bind off center 21 (23: 25) sts, P to end.

Complete to match first side, reversing shapings.

FRONT

Using size 10½ (7mm) needles, cast on 73 (79: 85) sts.

Work in fancy rib as given for Back for 16 rows, ending with **WS** facing for next row.

Row 17 (WS) P30 (33: 36) sts, [M1, P2] 6 times, M1, P to end. 80 (86: 92) sts.

Change to size 11 (8mm) needles.

Place cable panel

Row 1 (RS) P30 (33: 36), work next 20 sts as chart row 1 of cable panel, P to end.

Row 2 K30 (33: 36), work next 20 sts as chart row 2 of cable panel, K to end.

These 2 rows set position of cable panel with rev St st at sides.

Work even in patt, repeating the 24 row patt rep throughout, until Front matches Back to start of armhole shaping, ending with RS facing for next row.

Shape armholes

Keeping patt correct, bind off 4 sts at beg of next 2 rows. 72 (78: 84) sts.

Work even until 8 (8: 10) rows less have been worked than on Back to start of shoulder shaping, ending with RS facing for next row.

Shape neck

Next row (RS) P25 (27: 30) and turn, leaving rem sts on a holder.

Work each side of neck separately.

Dec 1 st at neck edge of next 4 rows, then on foll 1 (1: 2) alt rows. 20 (22: 24) sts.

Work 1 row, ending with RS facing for next row.

Shape shoulder

Bind off 10 (11: 12) sts at beg of next row.

Work 1 row.

Bind off rem 10 (11: 12) sts.

With RS facing, rejoin yarn to rem sts, bind off center 22 (24: 24) sts, P to end.

Complete to match first side, reversing shapings.

SLEEVES

Using size 10½ (7mm) needles, cast on 33 (35: 37) sts.

Row 1 (WS) Purl.

Row 2 P2 (3: 4), *sl 5 wyif, P3; rep from * to last 7 (8: 9) sts, sl 5 wyif, P2 (3: 4).

Row 3 K2 (3: 4), *P5, K3; rep from * to last 7 (8: 9) sts, P5, K2 (3: 4).

Row 4 P2 (3: 4), *K2, insert tip of right needle under strand of yarn of row 2 then K next st, K2, P3; rep from * to last 7 (8: 9) sts, K2, insert tip of right needle under strand of yarn of row 2 then K next st, K2, P2 (3: 4).

These 4 rows form fancy rib.

Work in fancy rib for 8 rows more, ending with WS facing for next row.

Row 13 (WS) Patt 11 (12: 13) sts, [M1, patt 2 sts] 6 times, M1, patt to end. 40 (42: 44) sts.

Change to size 11 (8mm) needles.

Place cable panel

Row 1 (RS) P10 (11: 12), work next 20 sts as chart row 1 of cable panel, P to end.

Row 2 K10 (11: 12), work next 20 sts as chart row 2 of cable panel, K to end.

These 2 rows set position of cable panel with rev St st at sides.

Cont as set, inc 1 st at each end of next row and every foll 4th row until there are 54 (60: 66) sts, then on every foll 6th row until there are 64 (68: 72) sts, taking inc sts into rev St st.

Work even until Sleeve measures 19¼ (19½: 20)in/ 49 (50: 51)cm from cast-on edge, ending with RS facing for next row.

Top of sleeve

Place markers at both ends of last row.

Work 6 rows more, ending with RS facing for next row. Bind off.

FINISHING

Press lightly on WS following instructions on yarn label and avoiding ribbing and cables.

Sew right shoulder seam.

Collar

With RS facing and using size 10½ (7mm) needles, pick up and knit 8 (9: 12) sts down left front neck edge, 15 (18: 18) sts along center front neck edge, 8 (9: 12) sts up right front neck edge, then 34 (37: 39) sts across back neck edge. 65 (73: 81) sts.

Starting with a P row, work in St st until Collar measures 2¾in/7cm from pick-up row, ending with RS of body facing for next row.

Now work in fancy rib as foll:

Row 1 (WS of Collar, RS of body) Purl.

Row 2 P2, *sl 5 wyif, P3; rep from * to last 7 sts, sl 5 wyif, P2.

Row 3 K2, *P5, K3; rep from * to last 7 sts, P5, K2.

Row 4 P2, *K2, insert tip of right needle under strand of yarn of row 2 then K next st, K2, P3; rep from * to last 7 sts, K2, insert tip of right needle under strand of yarn of row 2 then K next st, K2, P2.

These 4 rows form fancy rib.

Work in fancy rib for 16 rows more, ending with **WS** of Collar facing for next row.

Bind off in patt (on **WS**).

Sew left shoulder and Collar seam, reversing collar seam for turn-back. Matching sleeve markers to top of side seams and center of sleeve bound-off edge to shoulder seam, sew Sleeves to armholes. Sew side and sleeve seams.

Fair Isle stripe cushion

SARAH DALLAS

Size
The finished cushion cover fits a 18in/46cm square pillow form.

Yarns
5 x 50g/1¾oz balls of *Rowan Scottish Tweed DK* in main color **MC** (Storm Grey 004), and one ball each in **A** (Brilliant Pink 010), **B** (Lavender 005), **C** (Porridge 024), and **D** (Midnight 023)

Needles
Pair of size 5 (3.75mm) knitting needles
Pair of size 7 (4.5mm) knitting needles

Extras
18in/46cm square pillow form

Gauge
20 sts and 26 rows to 4in/10cm measured over St st using size 7 (4.5mm) needles *or size to obtain correct gauge.*

Abbreviations
See page 93.

Special note
When working patt in St st from chart, strand yarn not in use loosely across WS of work, weaving it in every 3 or 4 sts. Work odd-numbered rows as K rows, reading them from right to left, and even-numbered rows as P rows, reading them from left to right.

CUSHION COVER
Using size 5 (3.75mm) needles and A, cast on 91 sts.
Break off A and join in B.
Row 1 (RS) P1, *K1, P1; rep from * to end.
Row 2 K1, *P1, K1; rep from * to end.
These 2 rows form rib.
Work in rib for 4 rows more, ending with RS facing for next row.
Break off B and join in MC.
Change to size 7 (4.5mm) needles.
Beg with a K row, work in St st until Cover measures 12¼in/31cm from cast-on edge.
Place markers at both ends of last row.
Work even until Cover measures 4¾in/12cm from markers, ending with RS facing for next row.
Work first Fair Isle band
Join in B.
Rows 1 and 2 Using B, knit.
Joining in and breaking off C and D as required, work 9 rows from chart, ending with **WS** facing for next row.
Rows 12 and 13 Using B, purl.
Break off B.
Beg with a P row and using MC only, work even in St st until Cover measures 5½in/14cm from last row worked using B, ending with RS facing for next row.

Key
☐ C
■ D

Work second Fair Isle band

Join in A.

Rows 1 and 2 Using A, knit.

Joining in and breaking off C and D as required, work 9 rows from chart, ending with **WS** facing for next row.

Rows 12 and 13 Using A, purl.

Break off A.

Beg with a P row and using MC only, work even in St st until Cover measures 18in/46cm from markers, ending with RS facing for next row.

Place second set of markers at both ends of last row. Work even until Cover measures 10¼in/26cm from second set of markers, ending with **WS** facing for next row.

Break off MC and join in A.

Next row (WS) Purl.

Change to size 5 (3.75mm) needles.

Work in rib for 5 rows, ending with **WS** facing for next row.

Break off A and join in B.

Next row (RS) Knit.

Bind off purlwise.

FINISHING

Press lightly on WS following instructions on yarn label and avoiding ribbing.

With RS together, fold Cover level with first set of markers, then fold again level with second set of markers—cast-on and bound-off edges will overlap by about 5in/13cm. Sew row-end edges together to form side seams. Turn RS out and insert pillow form.

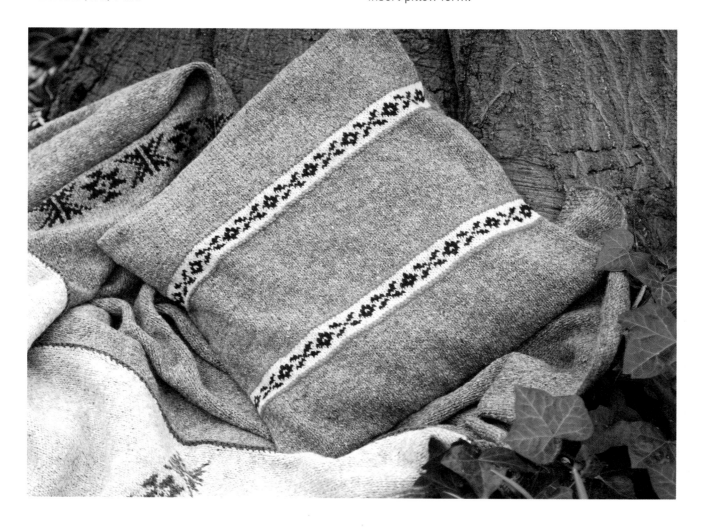

Chunky stripe cushion

SARAH DALLAS

Size

The finished cushion cover fits a 18in/46cm square
pillow form.

Yarns

3 x 100g/3½oz balls of Rowan *Scottish Tweed Chunky* in
main color **MC** (Lewis Grey 007), and one ball each in
A (Claret 013) and **B** (Midnight 023)

Needles

Pair of size 10½ (7mm) knitting needles
Pair of size 11 (8mm) knitting needles

Extras

18in/46cm square pillow form

Gauge

12 sts and 16 rows to 4in/10cm measured over
St st using size 11 (8mm) needles *or size to obtain
correct gauge*.

Abbreviations

See page 93.

Special note

When working patt in St st from chart, strand yarn not
in use loosely across WS of work, weaving it in every
3 or 4 sts. Work odd-numbered rows as K rows,
reading them from right to left, and even-numbered
rows as P rows, reading them from left to right.

CUSHION COVER

Using size 10½ (7mm) needles and A, cast on 53 sts.
Break off A and join in MC.
Row 1 (RS) P1, *K1, P1; rep from * to end.
Row 2 K1, *P1, K1; rep from * to end.
These 2 rows form rib.
Work in rib for 1 row more, ending with **WS** facing for
next row.
Change to size 11 (8mm) needles.
Beg with a P row, work in St st until Cover measures
12¼in/31cm from cast-on edge.
Place markers at both ends of last row.
Work even until Cover measures 6¼in/16cm from
markers, ending with RS facing for next row.
Work Fair Isle band
Join in A.
Rows 1 and 2 Using A, knit.
Break off A.
Joining in and breaking off B as required, work 19
rows from chart, ending with **WS** facing for next row.
Join in A.
Rows 22 and 23 Using A, purl.
Break off A.
Beg with a P row, work even in St st using MC until
Cover measures 18in/46cm from markers, ending with

Key
▫ MC

▪ B

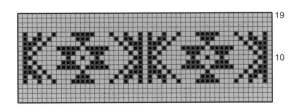

RS facing for next row.

Place second set of markers at both ends of last row.

Break off MC and join in B.

Work even until Cover measures 9in/23cm from second set of markers, ending with RS facing for next row.

Change to size 10½ (7mm) needles.

Work in rib for 4 rows, ending with RS facing for next row.

Break off B and join in A.

Using A, bind off in rib.

FINISHING

Press lightly on WS following instructions on yarn label and avoiding ribbing.

With RS together, fold Cover level with first set of markers, then fold again level with second set of markers—cast-on and bound-off edges will overlap by about 4¼in/11cm. Sew row-end edges together to form side seams. Turn RS out and insert pillow form.

Patchwork throw

CATHERINE TOUGH

Size

The finished throw measures 37½in/95cm by
65¼in/166cm.

Yarns

Rowan *Scottish Tweed DK*:

A	Grey Mist 001	8 x 50g/1¾oz balls
B	Storm Grey 004	4 x 50g/1¾oz balls
C	Purple Heather 030	2 x 50g/1¾oz balls
D	Autumn 029	2 x 50g/1¾oz balls
E	Herring 008	3 x 50g/1¾oz balls

Needles

Pair of size 7 (4.5mm) knitting needles
Cable needle

Gauge

20 sts and 26 rows to 4in/10cm measured over
St st using size 7 (4.5mm) needles *or size to obtain
correct gauge*.

Abbreviations

See page 93.

Special abbreviation

C6B = slip next 3 sts onto cable needle and leave at
back of work, K3, then K3 from cable needle.

FIRST SIDE STRIP

Using size 7 (4.5mm) needles and A, cast on 52 sts.

Row 1 (RS) [K4, P1] twice, [K6, P1, K4, P1] 3 times, K6.

Row 2 P6, [K1, P4, K1, P6] 3 times, [K1, P4] twice.

Rows 3 to 10 Rep rows 1 and 2 four times.

Row 11 [K4, P1] twice, [C6B, P1, K4, P1] 3 times, K6.

Row 12 Rep row 2.

Rows 13 to 20 Rep rows 1 and 2 four times.

These 20 rows form patt.

Work in patt until Strip measures 62¼in/158cm, ending with RS facing for next row.

Bind off in patt.

CENTER STRIP

Using size 7 (4.5mm) needles and B, cast on 77 sts.

Starting with a K row, work in St st for 9¾in/25cm, ending with RS facing for next row.

Break off B and join in C.

Cont in St st until Strip measures 18in/46cm from cast-on edge, ending with RS facing for next row.

Break off C and join in D.

Cont in St st until Strip measures 34½in/88cm from cast-on edge, ending with RS facing for next row.

Break off D and join in E.

Cont in St st until Strip measures 49½in/126cm from cast-on edge, ending with RS facing for next row.

Break off E and join in A.

Cont in St st until Strip measures 54¼in/138cm from cast-on edge, ending with RS facing for next row.

Break off A and join in B.

Cont in St st until Strip measures 62¼in/158cm from cast-on edge, ending with RS facing for next row.

Bind off.

SECOND SIDE STRIP

Using size 7 (4.5mm) needles and A, cast on 61 sts.

Row 1 (WS) Knit.

Row 2 *Insert tip of right needle knitwise into next st, wrap yarn around **both** needles by taking it under tip of right needle and over tip of left needle, then wrap yarn around tip of right needle **only** in the usual way as if to K a st, draw loop now on tip of right needle through st

and wrapped loop on left needle and drop st and loop off left needle, rep from * to end.

These 2 rows form lace patt.

Work in lace patt until Strip measures 31in/79cm, ending with RS facing for next row.

Break off A and join in C.

Starting with a K row, work in St st until Strip measures 39¾in/101cm from cast-on edge, ending with RS facing for next row.

Break off C and join in B.

Next row Knit.

Starting with row 1, cont in lace patt until Strip measures 62¼in/158cm from cast-on edge, ending with RS facing for next row.

Bind off.

FINISHING

Press lightly on WS following instructions on yarn label.

Using photograph as a guide and matching cast-on and bound-off edges, sew Side Strips to either side of Center Strip.

Borders (both alike)

Using size 7 (4.5mm) needles and E, cast on 8 sts.

Work in garter st (K every row) until Border, when slightly stretched, fits along entire cast-on (or bound-off) edge of joined Strips, ending with RS facing for next row.

Bind off.

Sew Borders to cast-on and bound-off edges of joined Strips as in photograph.

Child's jacket
CATHERINE TOUGH

Sizes

To fit age	1–2	2–3	4–5	years
To fit chest	20	22	24	in
	51	56	61	cm
Finished measurements				
Around chest	24	26½	28½	in
	61	67	72	cm
Length to shoulder	11¾	13½	15½	in
	30	34	39	cm
Sleeve seam	7¾	10¼	11¾	in
	20	26	30	cm

Yarns

4 (5: 6) x 50g/1¾oz balls of Rowan *Scottish Tweed DK* in **MC** (Herring 008)

1 (1: 1) x 25g/⁷⁄₈oz ball of Rowan *Scottish Tweed 4 ply* in **A** (Machair 002)

Needles

Pair of size 3 (3.25mm) knitting needles

Extras

3 buttons

Gauge

21 sts and 36 rows to 4in/10cm measured over garter st using MC and size 3 (3.25mm) needles *or size to obtain correct gauge.*

Abbreviations

See page 93.

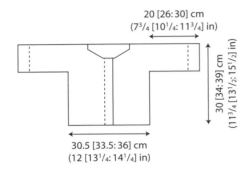

20 [26: 30] cm
(7³/₄ [10¹/₄: 11³/₄] in)

30 [34: 39] cm
(11³/₄ [13¹/₂: 15¹/₂] in)

30.5 [33.5: 36] cm
(12 [13¹/₄: 14¹/₄] in)

Special note

To work the "knit" cast-on when adding stitches for the sleeves, knit the first stitch on the left needle and transfer the stitch now on the right needle back onto the left needle. Continue adding stitches in this way.

POCKET

Using size 3 (3.25mm) needles and 2 strands of A held tog, cast on 7 sts.

Row 1 (RS) Inc in first st, K to last st, inc in last st.

Row 2 Purl.

Rep last 2 rows 4 (5: 6) times more, ending with RS facing for next row. 17 (19: 21) sts.

Starting with a K row, work in St st for 6 rows, ending with RS facing for next row.

Break off yarn and leave sts on a holder.

LEFT FRONT

Using size 3 (3.25mm) needles and 2 strands of A held tog, cast on 35 (38: 41) sts.

Starting with a K row, work in St st for 4 rows, ending with RS facing for next row.

Break off A and join in 1 strand of MC.

Work in garter st (K every row) until Left Front measures 7³/₄ (9: 10¹/₂)in/20 (23: 27)cm from first row using MC, ending with RS facing for next row.

Shape for sleeve

Using 1 strand of MC or 2 strands of A, cont as foll:

Next row (RS) Using the "knit" cast-on, cast on 48 (61: 70) sts in MC and 2 sts in A all onto left needle, then using A K2, using MC K to end. 85 (101: 113) sts.

Twisting yarns together where they meet on WS to avoid holes forming, patt as foll:

Next row Using MC K to last 2 sts, using A K2.

Next row Using A K2, using MC K to end.

These 2 rows form patt.

Cont in patt until Left Front measures 2 (2¹/₄: 2¹/₄)in/ 5 (6: 6)cm from sleeve cast-on edge, ending with **WS** facing for next row.

Shape neck

Keeping patt correct, bind off 7 (8: 7) sts at beg of next row. 78 (93: 106) sts.

Next row (RS) Patt to last 4 sts, K2tog, K2.

Next row K2, K2tog, patt to end. 76 (91: 104) sts.

Working all neck decreases as set by last 2 rows, dec 1 st at neck edge of next 12 rows, then on foll 0 (0: 1) alt row. 64 (79: 91) sts.

Work even until Left Front measures 4 (4¹/₂ : 4³/₄)in/ 10 (11: 12)cm from sleeve cast-on edge, ending with **WS** facing for next row.

Break off yarn and leave sts on a holder.

Mark positions for 3 buttons along left front opening edge—first to come level with row 25 of garter st section, last to come just below neck shaping and rem button evenly spaced between.

RIGHT FRONT

Using size 3 (3.25mm) needles and 2 strands of A held tog, cast on 35 (38: 41) sts.

Starting with a K row, work in St st for 4 rows, ending with RS facing for next row.

Break off A and join in 1 strand of MC.

Work in garter st (K every row) for 24 rows, ending with RS facing for next row.

Row 25 (RS) K2, K2tog, yo (to make a buttonhole), K to end.

Making 2 more buttonholes in this way to correspond with positions marked for buttons on Left Front and noting that no further reference will be made to buttonholes, cont as foll:

Work 24 (26: 30) rows, ending with **WS** facing for next row.

Place pocket

Next row (WS) K9, bind off next 17 (19: 21) sts

knitwise, K to end.

Next row K9 (10: 11), with RS facing K 17 (19: 21) sts from Pocket holder, K to end.

Work even until Right Front measures 7¾(9: 10½)in/ 20 (23: 27)cm from first row using MC, ending with **WS** facing for next row.

Shape for sleeve

Using 1 strand of MC or 2 strands of A, cont as foll:

Next row (WS) Using the "knit" cast-on, cast on 48 (61: 70) sts in MC and 2 sts in A all onto left needle, then using A K2, using MC K to end. 85 (101: 113) sts.

Twisting yarns together where they meet on WS to avoid holes forming, patt as foll:

Next row Using MC K to last 2 sts, using A K2.

Next row Using A K2, using MC K to end.

These 2 rows form patt.

Cont in patt until Right Front measures 2 (2¼: 2¼)in/ 5 (6: 6)cm from sleeve cast-on edge, ending with RS facing for next row.

Shape neck

Keeping patt correct, bind off 7 (8: 7) sts at beg of next row. 78 (93: 106) sts.

Working all neck decreases as set by Left Front, dec 1 st at neck edge of next 14 rows, then on foll 0 (0: 1) alt row. 64 (79: 91) sts.

Work even until Right Front measures 4 (4½: 4¾)in/ 10 (11: 12)cm from sleeve cast-on edge, ending with **WS** facing for next row.

Do NOT break off yarn.

BACK

With **WS** facing, patt 64 (79: 91) sts of Right Front, cast on 36 (38: 38) sts (for back neck) onto right needle, then patt 64 (79: 91) sts of Left Front.
164 (196: 220) sts.

Work even in patt as set (with 2 sts in garter st using A at **both** ends of rows) until Back measures 4 (4½: 4¾)in/10 (11: 12)cm from back neck cast-on edge, ending with RS facing for next row.

Shape sleeves

Bind off 50 (63: 72) sts at beg of next 2 rows. 64 (70: 76) sts.

Work even in garter st using MC only until Back measures 7¾ (9: 10½)in/20 (23: 27)cm from Sleeve bound-off edge, ending with RS facing for next row.

Break off MC and join in 2 strands of A.

Starting with a K row, work in St st for 4 rows, ending with RS facing for next row.

Bind off.

FINISHING

Press lightly on WS following instructions on yarn label.

Sew side and sleeve seams, reversing sleeve seam for first 2in/5cm for turn-back. Fold 1½in/4cm cuff to RS.

Sew on buttons.

Slip stitch pocket lining in place on WS.

Fair Isle socks

SARAH DALLAS

Size
The finished socks measure 11in/28cm from heel to toe (*adjustable*), 7in/18cm around foot, and 11in/28cm around calf.

Yarns
Version 1 (with pink edging):
3 x 25g/⁷/₈oz balls of Rowan *Scottish Tweed 4 ply* in main color **MC** (Grey Mist 001), and one ball each in **A** (Midnight 023), **B** (Lewis Grey 007), **C** (Porridge 024), and **D** (Brilliant Pink 010)
Version 2 (without pink edging):
3 x 25g/⁷/₈oz balls of Rowan *Scottish Tweed 4 ply* in main color **MC** (Grey Mist 001), and one ball each in **A** (Midnight 023), **B** (Lewis Grey 007), and **C** (Porridge 024)

Needles
Set of four size 3 (3.25mm) double-pointed knitting needles

Gauge
26 sts and 36 rounds to 4in/10cm measured over St st using size 3 (3.25mm) needles *or size to obtain correct gauge.*

Abbreviations
See page 93.

Special note
When working patt from chart, strand yarn not in use loosely across WS of work, weaving it in every 3 or 4 sts. Work ALL rounds as RS (knit) rounds, reading them from right to left.

Key
☐ MC
■ B
☐ C
■ A

12 st patt rep

14

10

SOCK (make 2)

Version 1 only

Using size 3 (3.25mm) double-pointed needles and D, cast on 72 sts, distributing them evenly over 3 needles. Break off D and join in B.

Round 1 (RS) *K1, P1; rep from * to end.

This round forms rib.

Work in rib for 9 rounds more, ending with RS facing for next row.

Break off B and join in MC.

Version 2 only

Using size 3 (3.25mm) double-pointed needles and A, cast on 72 sts, distributing them evenly over 3 needles. Break off A and join in MC.

Round 1 (RS) *K1, P1; rep from * to end.

This round forms rib.

Work in rib for 9 rounds more, ending with RS facing for next row.

Both versions

Joining in A, B, and C as required, repeating the 12 st patt rep 6 times around each round, work from chart as foll:

Work rounds 1–14 of chart.

Break off contrasting yarns and cont using MC only.

Round 15 (RS) Knit.

This round forms St st.

Work in St st for 19 rounds more.

Round 35 K2, K2tog, K to last 4 sts, skp, K2. 70 sts.

Work 4 rounds.

Rep last 4 rounds 8 times more, then round 35 again. 52 sts.

Work even until Sock measures 11in/28cm from cast-on edge.

Break off yarn.

Shape heel

Slip first and last 13 sts of next round onto a holder, leaving center 26 sts on needle.

Join in B and now working in **rows**, not rounds, work heel as foll:

Starting with a K row, work in St st for 20 rows, ending with RS facing for next row.

Next row (RS) K17, skp and turn.

Next row Sl 1, P8, P2tog and turn.

Next row Sl 1, K8, skp and turn.

Rep last 2 rows 6 times more.

Next row Sl 1, P8, P2tog. 10 sts.

Break off B.

With RS facing and using MC, with first needle pick up and knit 10 sts up first row-end edge of heel, and K 10 heel sts; with second needle pick up and knit 10 sts down second row-end edge of heel, then first 8 sts from holder; with third needle K rem 18 sts from holder. 56 sts.

Now working again in rounds of St st, cont as foll:

Next round (RS) K1, skp, K24, K2tog, K to end. 54 sts.

Work 1 round.

Next round (RS) K1, skp, K22, K2tog, K to end. 52 sts.

Work 1 round.

Next round (RS) K1, skp, K20, K2tog, K to end. 50 sts.

Work 1 round.

Next round (RS) K1, skp, K18, K2tog, K to end. 48 sts.

Work even in rounds of St st until Sock measures 7in/18cm (*or required length*) from heel pick-up row.

Shape toe

Break off MC and join in B.

Round 1 and every foll alt round Knit.

Round 2 [K1, skp, K18, K2tog, K1] twice. 44 sts.

Round 4 [K1, skp, K16, K2tog, K1] twice. 40 sts.

Round 6 [K1, skp, K14, K2tog, K1] twice. 36 sts.

Round 8 [K1, skp, K12, K2tog, K1] twice. 32 sts.

Round 10 [K1, skp, K10, K2tog, K1] twice. 28 sts.

Round 11 Rep round 1.

Bind off.

FINISHING

Press lightly on WS following instructions on yarn label and avoiding ribbing.

Sew toe seam.

Cabled blanket coat

SARAH DALLAS

Sizes

	XS–S	M–L	XL–XXL	
To fit bust	32–34	36–38	40–42	in
	81–86	91–97	102–107	cm
Finished measurements				
Around bust	59¾	63¼	67	in
	152	161	170	cm
Length to shoulder	20½	21¼	22	in
	52	54	56	cm
Sleeve seam	17	17¼	17¾	in
	43	44	45	cm

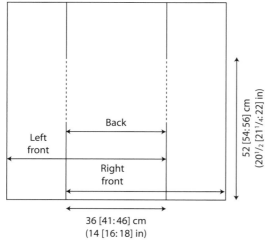

52 [54:56] cm
(20½ [21¼:22] in)

36 [41:46] cm
(14 [16:18] in)

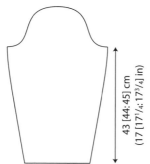

43 [44:45] cm
(17 [17¼:17¾ in)

Yarns

18 (19: 20) x 50g/1¾oz balls of Rowan *Scottish Tweed DK* in main color **MC** (Celtic Mix 022) and one ball in **A** (Midnight 023)

Needles

Pair of size 5 (3.75mm) knitting needles
Pair of size 7 (4.5mm) knitting needles
Cable needle

Gauge

21½ sts and 30 rows to 4in/10cm measured over patt using size 7 (4.5mm) needles *or size to obtain correct gauge.*

Abbreviations

See page 93.

Special abbreviation

C8B = slip next 4 sts onto cable needle and leave at back of work, K4, then K4 from cable needle.

BODY

The body is worked in one piece, starting at right front opening edge.
Using size 5 (3.75mm) needles and A, cast on 162 (166: 170) sts.
Break off A and join in MC.
Row 1 (RS) K2, *P2, K2; rep from * to end.
Row 2 P2, *K2, P2; rep from * to end.
These 2 rows form rib.
Work in rib for 9 rows more, ending with **WS** facing for next row.
Row 12 (WS) P2, K2, P2, K2tog, rib to end.
161 (165: 169) sts.

Change to size 7 (4.5mm) needles.

Now work in patt as foll:

Row 1 (RS) [K2, P2] 7 (8: 9) times, K2, *[P1, K1] twice, P2, K8, P1; rep from * to last 11 sts, [P1, K1] twice, P1, K2, P2, K2.

Row 2 P2, K2, P2, *[K1, P1] twice, K2, P8, K1; rep from * to last 35 (39: 43) sts, [K1, P1] twice, K1, [P2, K2] 7 (8: 9) times, P2.

Rows 3 to 6 Rep rows 1 and 2 twice.

Row 7 [K2, P2] 7 (8: 9) times, K2, *[P1, K1] twice, P2, C8B, P1; rep from * to last 11 sts, [P1, K1] twice, P1, K2, P2, K2.

Row 8 Rep row 2.

Rows 9 to 12 Rep rows 1 and 2 twice.

These 12 rows form patt.

Cont in patt until Body measures 22¾ (23½: 24½)in/ 58 (60: 62)cm from cast-on edge, ending with RS facing for next row.

**Shape armhole

Next row (RS) Patt 49 sts placing red marker on last of these sts, bind off next 56 (58: 60) sts, patt to end placing blue marker on first of these sts.

Next row Patt 56 (58: 60) sts, cast on 56 (58: 60) sts onto right needle, patt to end. 161 (165: 169) sts.**

Work even until Body measures 14 (16: 18)in/36 (41: 46)cm from armhole, ending with RS facing for next row.

Rep from ** to ** once more.

Work even until Body measures 20¾ (21½: 22½)in/ 53 (55: 57)cm from second armhole, ending with **WS** facing for next row.

Next row (WS) P2, K2, P2, inc in next st, rib to end. 162 (166: 170) sts.

Work in rib as given for cast-on edge for 12 rows, ending with RS facing for next row.

Break off MC and join in A.

Bind off.

SLEEVES

Using size 5 (3.75mm) needles and A, cast on 50 (54: 54) sts.

Break off A and join in MC.

Work in rib as given for Body for 2¾in/7cm, ending with RS facing for next row.

Change to size 7 (4.5mm) needles.

Cont in rib, shaping sides by inc 1 st at each end of next row and every foll 6th row to 70 (72: 84) sts, then on every foll 8th row until there are 80 (84: 88) sts, taking inc sts into rib.

Work even until Sleeve measures 17 (17¼: 17¾)in/ 43 (44: 45)cm from cast-on edge, ending with RS facing for next row.

Shape top of sleeve

Keeping rib correct, bind off 3 (4: 5) sts at beg of next 2 rows. 74 (76: 78) sts.

Dec 1 st at each end of next 7 rows, then on every foll alt row until 22 sts rem.

Work 1 row, ending with RS facing for next row.

Bind off rem 22 sts.

FINISHING

Press lightly on WS following instructions on yarn label.

Sew sleeve seams. Matching top of sleeve seam to blue (underarm) marker and center of sleeve bound-off edge to red (shoulder) marker, sew Sleeves to armholes.

Textured scarf

WENDY BAKER

Size

The finished scarf measures 11in/28cm by
55½in/141cm.

Yarns

4 x 25g/⅞oz balls of Rowan *Scottish Tweed 4 ply* in
main color **MC** (Celtic Mix 022), and 2 balls each in
A (Herring 008) and **B** (Winter Navy 021)

Needles

Pair of size 3 (3.25mm) knitting needles

Gauge

28 sts and 41 rows to 4in/10cm measured over
patt using size 3 (3.25mm) needles *or size to obtain
correct gauge.*

Abbreviations

See page 93.

SCARF

Using size 3 (3.25mm) needles and MC, cast on 79 sts.
Row 1 (RS) K1, *P1, K1; rep from * to end.
Row 2 Rep row 1.
These 2 rows form seed st.
Work in seed st for 12 rows more, ending with RS
facing for next row.
Using a separate ball of yarn for each block of color
and twisting yarns together on WS where they meet to
avoid holes forming, work in diamond patt as foll:
Row 1 (RS) Using MC seed st 9 sts, using A K1, [P1,
K9, P1, K1] 5 times, using MC seed st 9 sts.
Row 2 Using MC seed st 9 sts, using A K1, [P1, K1, P7,
K1, P1, K1] 5 times, using MC seed st 9 sts.
Row 3 Using MC seed st 9 sts, K1, *P1, K1, P1, K5, [P1,

K1] twice; rep from * 4 times more, seed st 9 sts.
Row 4 Using MC seed st 9 sts, P1, *[P1, K1] twice, P3,
K1, P1, K1, P2; rep from * 4 times more, seed st 9 sts.
Row 5 Using MC seed st 9 sts, using A K1, *K2, [P1,
K1] 3 times, P1, K3; rep from * 4 times more, using MC
seed st 9 sts.
Row 6 Using MC seed st 9 sts, using A P1, *P3, [K1,
P1] twice, K1, P4; rep from * 4 times more, using MC
seed st 9 sts.
Row 7 Using MC seed st 9 sts, K1, [K4, P1, K1, P1, K5]
5 times, seed st 9 sts.
Row 8 Using MC seed st 9 sts, P1, *P3, [K1, P1] twice,
K1, P4; rep from * 4 times more, seed st 9 sts.
Row 9 Rep row 5.
Row 10 Using MC seed st 9 sts, using A P1, *[P1, K1]
twice, P3, K1, P1, K1, P2; rep from * 4 times more,
using MC seed st 9 sts.
Row 11 Rep row 3.
Row 12 Using MC seed st 9 sts, K1, [P1, K1, P7, K1, P1,
K1] 5 times, seed st 9 sts.
These 12 rows form diamond patt and stripe sequence.
Cont as set until Scarf measures 10¼in/26cm from
cast-on edge, ending with RS facing for next row.
Break off A.
Work in diamond patt using MC **only** until Scarf
measures 18¾in/48cm from cast-on edge, ending with
WS facing for next row.
Next row (WS) Patt 9 sts, [inc in next st, patt 19 sts]
3 times, inc in next st, patt to end. 83 sts.
Using a separate ball of yarn for each block of color
and twisting yarns together on WS where they meet to
avoid holes forming, now work in block patt as foll:
Row 1 (RS) Using MC seed st 9 sts, using B K65, using
MC seed st 9 sts.
Row 2 Using MC seed st 9 sts, using B K5, [P5, K5] 12

times, using MC seed st 9 sts.

Rows 3 to 6 Rep rows 1 and 2 twice.

Row 7 Using MC seed st 9 sts, using B K65, using MC seed st 9 sts.

Row 8 Using MC seed st 9 sts, using B P5, [K5, P5] 12 times, using MC seed st 9 sts.

Rows 9 to 12 Rep rows 7 and 8 twice.

These 12 rows form block patt.

Work in block patt until Scarf measures 36½in/93cm from cast-on edge, dec 1 st at center of last row and ending with RS facing for next row. 82 sts.

Using a separate ball of yarn for each block of color and twisting yarns together on WS where they meet to avoid holes forming, now work in double seed st patt as foll:

Row 1 (RS) Using MC seed st 9 sts, using A [K2, P2] 16 times, using MC seed st 9 sts.

Row 2 Rep row 1.

Row 3 Using MC seed st 9 sts, using A [P2, K2] 16 times, using MC seed st 9 sts.

Row 4 Rep row 3.

These 4 rows form double seed st patt.

Work in double seed st patt until Scarf measures about 45½in/116cm from cast-on edge, ending after patt row 4 and with RS facing for next row.

Keeping double seed st patt correct, using a separate ball of yarn for each block of color and twisting yarns together on WS where they meet to avoid holes forming, now work in double seed st patt in stripes as foll:

Row 1 (RS) Using MC seed st 9 sts, [K2, P2] 16 times, seed st 9 sts.

Row 2 Rep row 1.

Row 3 Using MC seed st 9 sts, using A [P2, K2] 16 times, using MC seed st 9 sts.

Row 4 Rep row 3.

These 4 rows form striped double seed st patt. Work in striped double seed st patt until Scarf measures about 54¼in/138cm from cast-on edge, ending after patt row 3 and with **WS** facing for next row.

Next row (WS) Using MC seed st 9 sts, using A patt 9 sts, [work 2 tog, patt 20 sts] twice, work 2 tog,

patt 9 sts, using MC seed st 9 sts. 79 sts.

Break off A and cont using MC **only**.

Work in seed st for 14 rows, ending with RS facing for next row.

Bind off in seed st.

FINISHING

Press lightly on WS following instructions on yarn label.

Tie shrug

SARAH DALLAS

Sizes

	XS–M	L–XXL	
To fit bust	32–36	38–42	in
	81–91	97–107	cm
Finished measurements			
Width, excluding ties	39¼	43¼	in
	100	110	cm
Length	15¼	15¼	in
	39	39	cm

Yarn

9 (11) x 25g/⁷/₈oz balls of Rowan *Scottish Tweed 4 ply* in Heath 014

Needles

Pair of size 8 (5mm) knitting needles
Pair of size 13 (9mm) knitting needles

Gauge

11 sts and 28 rows to 4in/10cm measured over patt using 2 strands of yarn and size 13 (9mm) needles *or size to obtain correct gauge.*

Abbreviations

See page 93.

Special abbreviation

K1 below = K into next st 1 row below and at same time slip off st above.

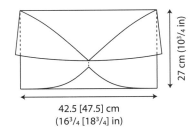

42.5 [47.5] cm
(16³/₄ [18³/₄] in)

27 cm (10³/₄ in)

MAIN SECTION

Using size 13 (9mm) needles and 2 strands of yarn held tog, cast on 93 (105) sts loosely.
Row 1 (RS) K2, *P1, K1; rep from * to last st, K1.
Now work in patt as foll:
Row 2 (WS) Sl 1, *P1, K1 below; rep from * to last 2 sts, P1, K1.
Row 3 Sl 1, *K1 below, P1; rep from * to last 2 sts, K1 below, K1.
Rows 2 and 3 form patt.
Work in patt for 20 rows more.
Change to size 8 (5mm) needles.
Next row (WS) K1, *P1, K1; rep from * to end.
Next row K1, *K1, P1; rep from * to last 2 sts, K2.
Last 2 rows form rib.
Work in rib for 2 rows more.
Change to size 13 (9mm) needles.
Work in patt for 20 rows.
Change to size 8 (5mm) needles.
Work in rib for 4 rows.
Change to size 13 (9mm) needles.
Work in patt for 18 rows.
Change to size 8 (5mm) needles.
Work in rib for 4 rows.
Change to size 13 (9mm) needles.
Work in patt for 16 rows.
Change to size 8 (5mm) needles.

Work in rib for 4 rows.

Change to size 13 (9mm) needles.

Work in patt for 12 rows.

Change to size 8 (5mm) needles.

Work in rib for 8 rows, ending with **WS** facing for next row.

Bind off in rib.

END SECTIONS AND TIES (both alike)

With RS facing, using size 13 (9mm) needles and 2 strands of yarn held tog, pick up and knit 58 sts along one row-end edge of Main Section.

Row 1 (WS) [P2tog] 29 times. 29 sts.

Place marker on center st of last row.

Row 2 K to within 1 st of marked st, sl 1, K2tog (marked st is first of these 2 sts), psso, K to end. 27 sts.

Row 3 K4, P to last 4 sts, K4.

Rep rows 2 and 3 nine times more. 9 sts.

Shape tie

Next row (RS) K2, yo, skp, K1, K2tog, yo, K2.

Next row K2, P2tog, yo, P1, yo, K2tog, K1.

Rep last 2 rows until Tie measures 11in/28cm, ending with RS facing for next row.

Bind off.

FINISHING

Press lightly on WS following instructions on yarn label.

Collared jacket

WENDY BAKER

Sizes

	S–M	L–XL	XXL–XXXL	
To fit chest	38–40	42–44	46–48	in
	97–102	107–112	117–122	cm

Finished measurements

	S–M	L–XL	XXL–XXXL	
Around chest	43¼	47¼	51	in
	110	120	130	cm
Length to shoulder	29	30	30¾	in
	74	76	78	cm
Sleeve seam	21¼	21½	22	in
	54	55	56	cm

Yarns

8 (9: 10) x 100g/3½oz balls of Rowan *Scottish Tweed Aran* in main color **MC** (Lovat 033) and one ball in **A** (Machair 002)

Needles

Pair of size 9 (5.5mm) knitting needles

Extras

4 buttons

Gauge

16 sts and 23 rows to 4in/10cm measured over St st using size 9 (5.5mm) needles *or size to obtain correct gauge*.

Abbreviations

See page 93.

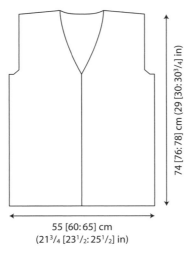

55 [60:65] cm
(21³/₄ [23¹/₂: 25¹/₂] in)

74 [76:78] cm (29 [30:30³/₄] in)

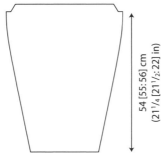

54 [55:56] cm
(21¹/₄ [21¹/₂: 22] in)

BACK

Using size 9 (5.5mm) needles and MC, cast on 88 (96: 104) sts.

Starting with a K row, work in St st until Back measures 19¹/₂ (20: 20¹/₂)in/50 (51: 52)cm from cast-on edge, ending with RS facing for next row.

Shape armholes

Bind off 3 (4: 5) sts at beg of next 2 rows. 82 (88: 94) sts.

Next row (RS) K1, skp, K to last 3 sts, K2tog, K1. 80 (86: 92) sts.

Working all armhole decreases as set by last row, dec 1 st at each end of 2nd row and foll 2 (3: 4) alt rows. 74 (78: 82) sts.

Work even until armhole measures 9 (9¹/₂: 9³/₄)in/ 23 (24: 25)cm, ending with RS facing for next row.

Shape back neck

Next row (RS) K25 (26: 27) and turn, leaving rem sts on a holder.

Work each side of neck separately.

Dec 1 st at neck edge of next row, ending with RS facing for next row. 24 (25: 26) sts.

Shape shoulder

Bind off 11 (12: 12) sts at beg and dec 1 st at end of next row.

Work 1 row.

Bind off rem 12 (12: 13) sts.

With RS facing, rejoin yarn to rem sts, bind off center 24 (26: 28) sts, K to end.

Complete to match first side, reversing shapings.

POCKET LININGS (make 2)

Using size 9 (5.5mm) needles and A, cast on 28 sts.

Starting with a K row, work in St st for 40 rows, ending with RS facing for next row.

Break off yarn and leave sts on a holder.

RIGHT FRONT

Using size 9 (5.5mm) needles and MC, cast on 40 (44: 48) sts.

Starting with a K row, work in St st for 4 rows, ending with RS facing for next row.

Row 5 (RS) Cast on 8 sts onto left needle and work [K1, P1] 4 times across these 8 sts, K to end. 48 (52: 56) sts.

Row 6 P to last 8 sts, [P1, K1] 4 times.

Row 7 [K1, P1] 4 times, K to end.

Rows 6 and 7 set the sts—with 8 sts in seed st at front opening edge and all other sts in St st.

Work as set for 37 rows more, ending with RS facing for next row.

Place pocket

Row 45 (RS) [K1, P1] 4 times, K6 (8: 10), slip next 28 sts onto a holder, then K across 28 sts of first Pocket Lining, K6 (8: 10).

Work even until Right Front matches Back to start of armhole shaping, ending with RS facing for next row.

Shape collar

Next row (RS) Inc in first st (for collar increase), seed st 7 sts, place marker on needle, K to end. 49 (53: 57) sts.

Working all collar increases as set by last row and

taking collar inc sts into seed st, cont as foll:

Shape armhole

Bind off 3 (4: 5) sts at beg of next row. 46 (49: 52) sts.

Shape front slope

Next row (RS) Seed st to marker, slip marker onto right needle, skp (for front slope decrease), K to last 3 sts, K2tog (for armhole decrease), K1. 44 (47: 50) sts.

Working all armhole and front slope decreases and collar increases as now set, cont as foll:

Dec 1 st at armhole edge of 2nd row and foll 2 (3: 4) alt rows **and at same time** dec 1 st at front slope edge of 4th row and foll 0 (4th: 4th) row **and at same time** inc 1 st at collar edge of 4th row and foll 0 (0: 6th) row. 41 (42: 45) sts.

Now keeping armhole edge straight, dec 1 st at front slope edge of 2nd (4th: 2nd) row and 7 (7: 8) foll 4th rows **and at same time** inc 1 st at collar edge of 4th (2nd: 6th) row and 5 (5: 4) foll 6th rows. 39 (40: 41) sts.

Work 5 (5: 1) rows, ending with RS facing for next row.

Shape revers

Next row (RS) Bind off 7 sts and return st on right needle to left needle, cast on 9 sts onto left needle and work these 9 sts in seed st, patt to end. 41 (42: 43) sts.

Work even until Right Front matches Back to start of **shoulder** shaping (this is 2 rows **after** start of back neck shaping), ending with RS facing for next row.

Work 1 row, ending with **WS** facing for next row.

Shape shoulder

Bind off 11 (12: 12) sts at beg of next row, then 12 (12: 13) sts at beg of foll alt row. 18 sts.

Shape back collar extension

Next row (RS of Front, WS of Collar) Seed st 12 sts and turn.

Next row Sl 1, seed st to end.

Work in seed st across all sts for 6 rows.

Rep last 8 rows until shorter row-end edge of collar extension measures 3½ (3¾: 4)in/9 (9.5: 10)cm.

Bind off in seed st.

Mark positions for 4 buttons along right front opening edge—first to come level with row 11, last to come just below start of front slope shaping, and rem 2 buttons evenly spaced between.

LEFT FRONT

Using size 9 (5.5mm) needles and MC, cast on 40 (44: 48) sts.

Starting with a K row, work in St st for 5 rows, ending with **WS** facing for next row.

Row 6 (WS) Cast on 8 sts onto left needle and work [K1, P1] 4 times across these 8 sts, P to end. 48 (52: 56) sts.

Row 7 K to last 8 sts, [P1, K1] 4 times.

Row 8 [K1, P1] 4 times, P to end.

Rows 7 and 8 set the sts—with 8 sts in seed st at front opening edge and all other sts in St st.

Work as set for 2 rows more, ending with RS facing for next row.

Row 11 (RS) Patt to last 6 sts, work 2 tog, [yo] twice, work 2 tog (to make a buttonhole), seed st 2 sts.

Row 12 Seed st 3 sts, [P1, K1] into double yo of previous row, patt to end.

Working 3 more buttonholes as set by last 2 rows to correspond with positions marked for buttons on Right Front and noting that no further reference will be made to buttonholes, cont as foll:

Work 32 rows more, ending with RS facing for next row.

Place pocket

Row 45 (RS) K6 (8: 10), slip next 28 sts onto a holder, then K across 28 sts of second Pocket Lining, K6 (8: 10), [P1, K1] 4 times.

Work even until Left Front matches Back to start of armhole shaping, ending with RS facing for next row.

Shape collar and armhole

Next row (RS) Bind off 3 (4: 5) sts, K to last 8 sts, place marker on needle, seed st 7 sts, inc in last st (for collar increase). 46 (49: 52) sts.

Working all collar increases as set by last row and taking collar inc sts into seed st, cont as foll:

Work 1 row.

Shape front slope

Next row (RS) K1, skp (for armhole decrease), K to within 2 sts of marker, K2tog (for front slope decrease), slip marker onto right needle, seed st to end. 44 (47: 50) sts.

Working all armhole and front slope decreases and collar increases as now set, cont as foll:

Dec 1 st at armhole edge of 2nd row and foll 2 (3: 4) alt rows **and at same time** dec 1 st at front slope edge of 4th row and foll 0 (4th: 4th) row **and at same time** inc 1 st at collar edge of 4th row and foll 0 (0: 6th) row. 41 (42: 45) sts.

Now keeping armhole edge straight, dec 1 st at front slope edge of 2nd (4th: 2nd) row and 7 (7: 8) foll 4th rows **and at same time** inc 1 st at collar edge of 4th (2nd: 6th) row and 5 (5: 4) foll 6th rows. 39 (40: 41) sts.

Work 4 (4: 0) rows, ending with **WS** facing for next row.

Shape revers

Next row (WS) Bind off 7 sts and return st on right needle to left needle, cast on 9 sts onto left needle and work these 9 sts in seed st, patt to end. 41 (42: 43) sts.

Work even until Left Front matches Back to start of **shoulder** shaping (this is 2 rows **after** start of back neck shaping), ending with RS facing for next row.

Shape shoulder

Bind off 11 (12: 12) sts at beg of next row, then 12 (12: 13) sts at beg of foll alt row. 18 sts.

Shape back collar extension

Next row (WS of Front, RS of Collar) Seed st 12 sts and turn.

Next row Sl 1, seed st to end.

Work in seed st across all sts for 5 rows.

Rep last 8 rows until shorter row-end edge of collar extension measures 3½ (3¾: 4)in/9 (9.5: 10)cm.

Bind off in seed st.

SLEEVES

Using size 9 (5.5mm) needles and MC, cast on 40 (42: 44) sts.

Starting with a K row, work in St st for 16 rows, ending with RS facing for next row.

Row 17 (RS) K3, M1, K to last 3 sts, M1, K3. 42 (44: 46) sts.

Working all increases as set by last row, inc 1 st at each end of 6th row and every foll 6th row until there are 66 (72: 80) sts.

S–M and L–XL sizes only

Inc 1 st at each end of every foll 8th row until there are 72 (76) sts.

All sizes

Work even until Sleeve measures 21¼ (21½: 22)in/ 54 (55: 56)cm from cast-on edge, ending with RS facing for next row.

Shape top of sleeve

Place markers at both ends of last row.

Work 4 (6: 8) rows more, ending with RS facing for next row.

Working all decreases in same way as for Back armhole decreases, dec 1 st at each end of next row and foll 3 (4: 5) alt rows.

Work 1 row, ending with RS facing for next row.

Bind off rem 64 (66: 68) sts.

FINISHING

Press lightly on WS following instructions on yarn label.

Sew shoulder seams. Sew center back (bound-off edge) seam of collar extensions, then sew one edge to back neck. Matching sleeve markers to top of side seams and center of sleeve bound-off edge to shoulder seam, sew Sleeves to armholes. Sew side and sleeve seams, reversing seams for final 4 rows of roll-back edging.

Pocket tops (both alike)

Slip 28 pocket sts onto size 9 (5.5mm) needles and rejoin MC with RS facing.

Starting with a K row, work in St st for 2 rows, ending with RS facing for next row.

Bind off.

Sew Pocket Linings in place on inside, then neatly sew down ends of Pocket Tops. Sew on buttons.

USEFUL INFORMATION

The following notes will help you to knit the garments in this book successfully.

GAUGE

Obtaining the correct gauge is the factor that can make the difference between a garment that fits and one that does not. It controls both the shape and size of a knitted garment, so any variation, however slight, can distort the finished size. Different designers feature in our books and it is their gauge, given at the start of each pattern, that you must match.

To check this against your own gauge, we recommend that you knit a square in pattern and/or stockinette stitch (depending on the pattern instructions) of perhaps 5 to 10 more stitches and 5 to 10 more rows than those given in the gauge note. Mark out the central 4in (10cm) square with pins. If you have too many stitches to 4in (10cm), try again using larger sized needles. If you have too few stitches to 4in (10cm), try again using smaller sized needles.

Once you have achieved the correct gauge, your garment will be knitted to the measurements indicated in the size diagram shown with the pattern.

SIZING

The instructions in each pattern are given for the smallest size. The figures in parentheses are for the larger sizes. Where there is one set of figures only, it applies to all sizes.

All garment patterns include "ease" to allow for a comfortable fit. The finished measurement around the bust/chest of the knitted garment is given at the start of each pattern and includes this ease. The size diagram shows the finished width of the garment at the underarm, and it is this measurement that you should use to choose an appropriate size.

A useful tip is to measure one of your own garments that fits comfortably and choose a size that is similar. Having chosen a size based on width, look at the corresponding length for that size; if you are not happy with the total length that we recommend, adjust your own garment before beginning your armhole shaping—any adjustment after this point will mean that your sleeve will not fit into your garment easily; and don't forget to take your adjustment into account if there is any side-seam shaping.

Finally, look at the sleeve length; the size diagram shows the finished sleeve measurement, taking into account any top-arm insertion length. Measure your body between the center of your neck and your wrist, this measurement should correspond to half the garment width plus the sleeve length. Again, your sleeve length may be adjusted, but remember to take into consideration your sleeve increases if you do adjust the length—you must increase more frequently than the pattern states to shorten your sleeve, less frequently to lengthen it.

CHART NOTE

Many of the patterns in the book are worked from charts. Each square on a chart represents a stitch and each line of squares represents a row of knitting. Each color used is given a different letter and these are shown in the materials section, or in the key alongside the chart of each pattern.

When working from the charts, read odd-numbered rows (K) from right to left and even-numbered rows (P) from left to right, unless otherwise stated.

KNITTING WITH MORE THAN ONE COLOR

There are two main methods of working color into a knitted fabric: the intarsia and Fair Isle techniques. The first method produces a single thickness of fabric and is usually used where a color is only required in a particular area of a row. Where a repeating pattern is created across the row, the Fair Isle technique is usually used.

Intarsia technique

For this technique, cut lengths of yarn for each motif or block of color used in a row. Then join in the various colors at the appropriate position in the row, linking one color to the next by twisting them around each other where they meet on the wrong side to avoid gaps.

All yarn ends can then either be darned along the color join lines after each motif is completed, or can be "knitted-in" on the wrong side of the knitting as each color is worked into the pattern. This is done in much the same way as "weaving-in" yarns when working the Fair Isle technique and saves time darning-in ends.

It is essential that the gauge is noted for intarsia, because this may vary from the plain stockinette stitch gauge if both are used in the same pattern.

Fair Isle technique

When two or three colors are worked repeatedly across a row, strand the yarn not in use loosely behind the stitches being worked.

If you are working with more than two colors, treat the "floating" yarns as if they were one yarn and always spread the stitches to their correct width to keep them elastic.

It is advisable not to carry the stranded or "floating" yarns over more than three stitches at a time, but to weave them under and over the color you are working to catch the "floating" yarns into the back of the work.

SLIP-STITCH EDGINGS

When a row end edge forms the actual finished edge of a garment, a slip-stitch edging makes a neat edge.

To work a slip-stitch edging at the end of a right side row, work across the row until there is one stitch left on the left needle. Pick up the loop lying between the needles and place this loop on the right needle. (Note that this loop does NOT count as a stitch and is not included in any stitch counts.) Now slip the last stitch knitwise with the yarn at the back of the work. At the beginning of the next row, purl together the first (slipped) stitch with the picked-up loop.

To work a slip-stitch edging at the end of a wrong side row, work across the row until there is one stitch left on the left needle. Pick up the loop lying between the needles and place this loop on the right needle. (Note that this loop does NOT count as a stitch and is not included in any stitch counts.) Now slip the last stitch purlwise with the yarn at the front of the work. At the beginning of the next row, knit together through the back of the loop the first (slipped) stitch with the picked-up loop.

FINISHING INSTRUCTIONS

After you have worked for hours knitting a garment, it would be a pity to spoil it by not taking enough care with the pressing and finishing process. Follow these tips for a truly professional-looking garment.

PRESSING

Block out each piece of knitting and, following the instructions on the yarn label, press the garment pieces, avoiding any ribbing.

Take special care to press the edges, as this will make sewing the seams both easier and neater. If the yarn label indicates that the fabric should not be pressed, then covering the blocked out fabric with a damp white cotton cloth and leaving it to stand will have the desired effect.

Darn in all ends neatly along the selvage edge or a color join, as appropriate.

SEWING SEAMS

When sewing the pieces together, remember to match areas of color and texture very carefully where they meet. Use backstitch or mattress stitch for all main knitting seams, and sew together ribbing and neckband seams with mattress stitch, unless otherwise stated.

CONSTRUCTION

Having completed the garment pieces, sew the seams in the order stated in the instructions. After sewing the shoulder seams, sew the top of the sleeve to the body of the garment using the method detailed in the pattern, referring to the appropriate guide:

Straight cast-off sleeves: Place the center of the bound-off edge of the sleeve at the shoulder seam. Sew the top of the sleeve to the back and front.

Square set-in sleeves: Place the center of the bound-off edge of the sleeve at the shoulder seam. Sew the top of the sleeve into the armhole, with the straight sides at the top of the sleeve forming a neat right-angle to the bound-off stitches at the armhole.

Shallow set-in sleeves: Place the center of the bound-off edge of the sleeve at the shoulder seam. Match the decreases at the beginning of the armhole shaping with the decreases at the top of the sleeve, and sew the sleeve cap to the armhole, easing in the shapings.

Set-in sleeves: Place the center of the bound-off edge of the sleeve at the shoulder seam. Sew in the sleeve, easing the sleeve cap into the armhole.

Lastly, slip stitch any pocket edgings and linings in place and sew on buttons to correspond with buttonholes.

ABBREVIATIONS

KNITTING ABBREVIATIONS

alt	alternate
beg	begin(ning)
cm	centimeter(s)
cont	continu(e)(ing)
dec	decreas(e)(ing)
foll	follow(s)(ing)
in	inch(es)
inc	increas(e)(ing)
K	knit
m	meters
M1	make one stitch by picking up horizontal loop before next stitch and knitting (or purling) into back of it
M1P	make one stitch by picking up horizontal loop before next stitch and purling into back of it
mm	millimeter(s)
P	purl
patt	pattern
psso	pass slipped stitch over
p2sso	pass 2 slipped stitches over
rem	remain(s)(ing)
rep	repeat(ing)
rev St st	reverse stockinette stitch (P all RS rows and K all WS rows)
RS	right side
skp	slip 1, knit 1, psso
sl 1	slip one stitch
st(s)	stitch(es)
St st	stockinette stitch (K all RS rows and P all WS rows)
tbl	through back of loop(s)
tog	together
WS	wrong side
yd	yard(s)
yo	yarn over (yarn around right needle to make a new stitch)
0	no stitches, times or rows for that size
[ ]	repeat instructions inside brackets as many times as instructed

CROCHET ABBREVIATIONS

Simple crochet has been used for edgings for a few garments in this book. US terminology has been used in the pattern instructions. The UK equivalents are given below

US		UK	
ch	chain	**ch**	chain
sc	single crochet	**dc**	double crochet
slip st	slip stitch	**ss**	slip stitch

ABOUT THE YARNS

Rowan Scottish Tweed Yarns (formerly known as Harris Yarns) are available in four weights: 4 ply, DK, Aran, and Chunky. The full range of colors is obtainable in 4 ply. The other weights come in some but not all of these colors. All the yarns are to be hand washed or can be dry cleaned at the cleaner's discretion.

For a store selling Rowan yarns near you, contact the distributor in your country or visit the Rowan UK website.

Rowan Scottish Tweed 4 ply

A lightweight 100 percent pure wool yarn
Ball size: 25g (7/8oz); about 120yd/110m per ball
Recommended gauge: 26-28 sts and 38-40 rows to 4in/10cm measured over St st using needle size 2-3 (3-3.25mm) needles

Rowan Scottish Tweed DK

A medium weight 100 percent pure wool yarn
Ball size: 50g (13/4oz); about 123yd/113m per ball.
Recommended gauge: 20-22 sts and 28-30 rows to 4in/10cm measured over St st using size 6 (4mm) needles

Rowan Scottish Tweed Aran

A thick 100 percent pure wool yarn
Ball size: 100g (31/2oz); about 186yd/170m per ball
Recommended gauge: 16 sts and 23rows to 4in/10cm measured over St st using size 8-9 (5-5.5mm) needles

Rowan Scottish Tweed Chunky

A chunky 100 percent pure wool yarn
Ball size: 100g (4oz); about 109yd/100m per ball.
Recommended gauge: 12 sts and 16 rows to 4in/10cm measured over St st using size 11 (8mm) needles

YARN DISTRIBUTORS

USA

Westminster Fibers Inc.,
4 Townsend West, Suite 8, Nashua, NH 03063.
Tel: +1 (603) 886-5041/5043.
E-mail: rowan@westminsterfibers.com

UK

Rowan Yarns,
Green Lane Mill, Holmfirth, West Yorkshire HD9 2DX.
Tel: 01484 681881.
E-mail: mail@knitrowan.com
www.knitrowan.com

AUSTRALIA

Australian Country Spinners,
314 Albert Street, Brunswick, Victoria 3056.
Tel: (03) 9380 3888.
E-mail: sales@auspinners.com.au

BELGIUM

Pavan,
Meerlaanstraat 73, B9860 Balegem (Oosterzele).
Tel: (32) 9 221 8594.
E-mail: pavan@pandora.be

CANADA

Diamond Yarn,
9697 St. Laurent, Montreal, Quebec H3L 2N1.
Tel: (514) 388 6188.
Diamond Yarn (Toronto),
155 Martin Ross, Unit 3, Toronto, Ontario M3J 2L9.
Tel: (416) 736-6111.
E-mail: diamond@diamondyarn.com

FINLAND

Coats Opti Oy,
Ketjutie 3, 04220 Kerava.
Tel: (358) 9 274 871.
Fax: (358) 9 2748 7330.
E-mail: coatsopti.sales@coats.com

FRANCE
Elle Tricot,
8 Rue du Coq, 67000 Strasbourg.
Tel: (33) 3 88 23 03 13.
E-mail: elletricot@agat.net
www.elletricote.com

GERMANY
Wolle & Design,
Wolfshovener Strasse 76,
52428 Julich-Stetternich. Tel: (49) 2461 54735.
E-mail: Info@wolleunddesign.de
www.wolleunddesign.de
Coats GMbH,
Eduardstrasse 44, D-73084 Salach.
Tel: (49) 7162/14-346. www.coatsgmbh.de

HOLLAND
de Afstap,
Oude Leliestraat 12, 1015 AW Amsterdam.
Tel: (31) 20 6231445.

HONG KONG
East Unity Co. Ltd.,
Unit B2, 7/F Block B, Kailey Industrial Centre,
12 Fung Yip Street, Chai Wan.
Tel: (852) 2869 7110.

ICELAND
Storkurinn,
Laugavegi 59, 101 Reykjavik.
Tel: (354) 551 8258. E-mail: malin@mmedia.is

ITALY
D.L. srl, Via Piave 24–26, 20016 Pero, Milan.
Tel: (39) 02 339 10 180.

JAPAN
Puppy Co Ltd.,
T151-0051, 3-16-5 Sendagaya, Shibuyaku, Tokyo.
Tel: (81) 3 3490 2827.
E-mail: info@rowan-jaeger.com

KOREA
Coats Korea Co. Ltd.,
5F Kuckdong B/D, 935-40 Bangbae-Dong, Seocho-Gu,
Seoul.
Tel: (82) 2 521 6262.
Fax: (82) 2 521 5181.

NORWAY
Coats Knappehuset A/S,
Postboks 63, 2801 Gjovik.
Tel: (47) 61 18 34 00.

SINGAPORE
Golden Dragon Store,
101 Upper Cross Street #02-51, People's Park Centre.
Tel: (65) 6 5358454.

SOUTH AFRICA
Arthur Bales PTY,
PO Box 44644, Linden 2104.
Tel: (27) 11 888 2401.

SPAIN
Oyambre,
Pau Claris 145, 80009 Barcelona.
Tel: (34) 670 011957.
E-mail: comercial@oyambreonline.com

SWEDEN
Wincent,
Norrtullsgatan 65, 113 45 Stockholm.
Tel: (46) 8 33 70 60.
E-mail: wincent@chello.se

TAIWAN
Laiter Wool Knitting Co. Ltd.,
10-1 313 Lane, Sec 3,
Chung Ching North Road, Taipei.
Tel: (886) 2 2596 0269.
Mon Cher Corporation,
9F No 117 Chung Sun First Road, Kaoshiung.
Tel: (886) 7 9711988.

ACKNOWLEDGMENTS

We would like to thank the following for their help with this book:

John Heseltine for photography (and Tara Heseltine for assisting), Anne Wilson for design, and Emma Freemantle for styling; Penny Hill, Eva Yates, and their teams for knitting; Sue Whiting, Stella Smith, and Marilyn Wilson for pattern writing and checking, and Sally Harding for proofreading.

Thanks also to Kate Buller, Ann Hinchcliffe, and Lee Wills at Rowan Yarns.

We are also grateful to JJ Locations (and Gloria Thompson) for locations; Models One and Storm for the models, Hannah and Bradley; and Astrid & Alice in Notting Hill, London, for lending garments for photography.